EROTIC ART
OF THE MASTERS
THE 18th, 19th & 20th CENTURIES

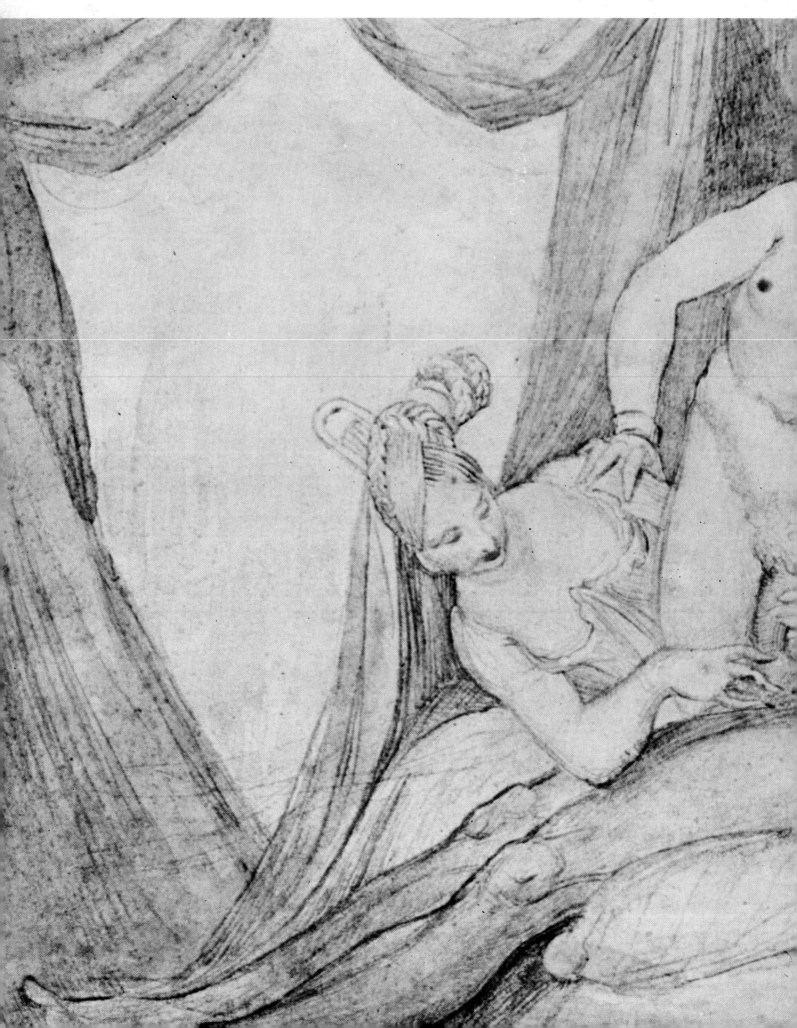

The 18th, 19th & 20th Centuries by BRADLEY SMITH

A Gemini-Smith, Inc. Book - Published by Mayflower Books

Consultants:
J.-M. Lo Duca
Lawrence Gichner
Henry Miller

Design: Bradley Smith and Don McQuiston
Photographs: Bradley Smith except as
credited in acknowledgments

CONTENTS

Introduction By Henry Miller

EROTIC ART IN THE 18th CENTURY

EROTIC ART IN THE 19th CENTURY

EROTIC ART IN THE 20th CENTURY

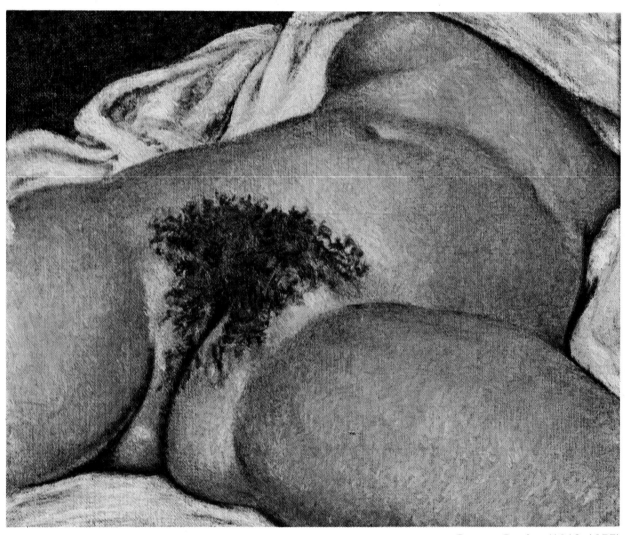

Gustave Courbet (1819-1877)

PREFACE

Because the great artists of the 18th, 19th and 20th centuries have been leaders in sexual enlightenment, modern erotic art has been liberated from many of the taboos and subterfuges of past generations. Out of the dark ages of repression, the dynamic energy of the art dealing with sex and love has finally come into the light. Paintings of great esthetic value, which have been hidden through the ages, have been freed from their self-appointed keepers. Now the artist can show directly—sometimes poetically, sometimes shockingly—sex and love, as human beings reveal themselves. No longer must the art of love be lost in symbolism.

Now the time has come for the people of the world to have an opportunity to view these works. This, therefore, is neither an art book masquerading as a sex book, nor is it a sex book masquerading as an art book. It does not deal with the psychology behind the erotic paintings of the great masters. Rather than attempting to tell why Degas painted his immortal brothel scenes or to explain Jean François Millet's interest in the daily toil of the farmer and, simultaneously, his joyous paintings of intercourse and masturbation performed in the haystacks by the same characters, and rather than dwelling on the vigorous explosion of sexual energy in Tassaert's "The Damned Woman," it is enough that the artists, who have devoted themselves to recording humanity's most useful and pleasurable pursuit, created the paintings that can be seen and enjoyed on these pages.

In the 18th century erotic painting often had both religious and political significance. In the 19th century the representation of sexual acts became influenced increasingly by the classical tradition in literature and in art. Finally, in the

20th century artists found it possible to freely show the affection of men and women, women and women, men and men in all the variations of pleasures that the human mind and instinct have practiced. Regardless of political, religious or economic crises, and no matter how much attention artists pay to war and politics, the intimate relations of humans through the ages have been the most important component in their paintings, drawings and sculpture.

Erotic painting has never been the exclusive province of socially or politically radical artists. Painters such as Degas, David and Daumier did not belong to the so-called Bohemian group of 19th century France. They were, along with many of their colleagues, conservatives. Yet, by viewing those of their works that deal with variations on a sexual theme, one can see they were liberal, even radical, for their time in their approach to sex in art. These artists played an important part in freeing painting from the hypocrisy of symbolism, although they are not numbered among the artists who were radicals politically, socially and artistically. Rodin, Toulouse-Lautrec, Vincent Van Gogh and Paul Gauguin were considered political and/or social radicals, yet in their erotic works they joined with the conservatives in their insistence on painting what they saw.

It would seem, then, that erotic art has never been determined by either the politics of the artist nor his social status. The interest of the artist in the visual aspects of sex is apparently universal. It would seem to follow that the creative impulse to paint has often been stimulated by relating to the fundamental act of creation. Sex—for pleasure or pain, not reproduction—was the source, the model in one way or another, of the greatest number of paintings produced by the artist and enjoyed by the viewer. The depiction of the acts of creation once used the mythological gods, showing them involved in the human aspects of sex. In the world of sex before the 18th century, the gods were given the aspect of humans, but since then humans have replaced gods.

Even though the question is unanswerable, some viewers will ask: "But why did the artists paint these pictures?" There are no simple answers. But, if it is remembered that artists are men and women with the same passions, illusions, dreams and fantasies that are happily the lot of almost everyone, there is a clue. And even when their erotic representations seem unreal or distressing, the sympathetic viewer will find compassion for the human condition within the artist's concept. The questions are easy to ask.

Does the expression of the artist's vision reflect his own longing? Does it mirror his agony in his attempt to understand his own relationship with sex? Does it reflect his knowledge, his understanding of the relationship of humans to one another? Is the artist's attitude toward life and love released in his creative work dealing with sex? The answers are indicated to the discerning viewer, who may see himself as well as the artist's meaning on these pages.

All of us, artists and non-artists as well, can learn from reaching toward the understanding of human sexuality that is shown in great paintings. Yet both the fantasies of sex and the realities are usually seen in fragmented forms. The fragments of eroticism may split apart into hetero-, homo- and solo sexual pleasures and, beneath the surface, all the fragments of human sexuality have been accepted in ancient and modern societies. The infinite variety of sexual pleasures, when viewed in the form of images created by great artists, represents a vital part of the world's sexual knowledge. The artist could visually translate the sense of touch, smell and taste. In this field he is all-powerful. Artists show impact, energy, vigor and potency through the way in which they depict our sexual needs and gratifications. It is sometimes possible to physically know complete sexual abandonment when viewing the outthrust arm and the widespread fingers of a woman in ecstasy as painted by Honoré Daumier.

Now to define erotic art as it is shown and spoken of in this book. The word "erotic" comes from *eros* or *erogenesis*, which in ancient Greece was synonymous with sexual love. Erotic art, then, means art that depicts sexual love or sexual desire. Erotic can be said to describe the dominance of the love instinct over the death instinct. Erotic art is used here to describe fertile, dynamic, vigorous art celebrating the sometimes poetic, disturbing, abstract, realistic joys of sex.

Erotic art is not pornography. Indeed, it would seem time to bury the word pornographic as a synonym for erotic. The meaning and the sound of the word go back to its Greek origins. The meaning of *porne* in Greek is prostitute or harlot. A government that was dominated by prostitutes, as was Rome in the 10th century, could be called a pornocracy. Pornography was in Greece a description of the manners of Greek harlots but, because of the lack of a better word, pornography has taken on different meanings at different times in different places. However, the drawings of Maillol, the sculpture of Rodin, the etchings of Degas and of Daumier, the erotic paintings of Picasso have nothing to do with a description of the manners of Greek or Roman whores. Their works, and that of all great artists, are erotic not pornographic.

Every man should have a choice as to his own definition of erotic art, for the different kinds of stimulation visualized in the painting, drawing and sculpture of affection, love, desire and sex are infinite. One man's or woman's lubricity may be another's lassitude. One person's interest is another's boredom. Whether this book is erotically stimulating will depend upon each individual's reaction. The criteria for the works selected for this volume have been: Is the painting or drawing a sensitive, dramatic, humorous, realistic or fantastic representation of the artist's creativity in dealing with the world of sex?

Bradley Smith

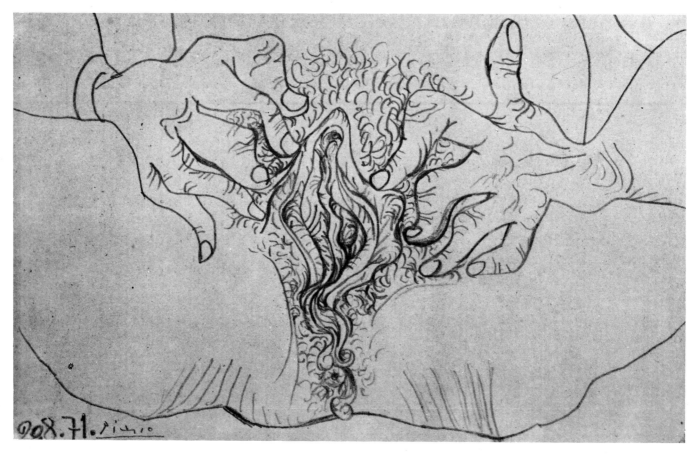

INTRODUCTION

Today we enjoy the freedom to read, read most anything, whether by a literary master or by a hack with a flair for using "dirty" words. Even the cinema permits us to observe couples performing the sex act. When it comes to sculpture and painting however there is still an aura of the forbidden connected with presenting them to the public. Monarchs, aristocrats and millionaires have always had access to these forbidden treasures of art. So has the Church and State. To be sure, these collections are not at the disposal of the general public. They are there, presumably, so that the religious and political leaders may warn the faithful of what not to read, what not to look at. The strange thing is that, so far as we know, none of the keepers of this unholy assortment of art has ever run amuck, has never become a rapist or a degenerate, which it is alleged might happen to the man in the street were he exposed to such works. The rich collector, the expert, the critic of art, the clergy, the censors might view such work without fear of moral derangement, but not the ordinary man. *L'homme moyen* was regarded as a potential sex maniac who had to be hedged in with all manner of restrictive prohibitions.

The selection of erotic paintings and sculpture in this book represents the work of esteemed artists. Their work has been admired, often venerated, by the critics and connoisseurs of their time. What then caused these eminent artists to stray afield, so to speak? Were they temporarily deranged, were they obsessed by sex, were they nasty, evil-minded individuals? In general they were not, as the body of their work testifies. They chose the erotic, much as the ordinary individual does, because it is an enduring and powerful element of life. The erotic as well as the occult, as I have said time and again, never cease to appeal, never fail to hold our attention. Yet for centuries the censors, whether lay or clerical, have tried to suppress what is pleasurable and stimulating to the senses—or the base appetites of man, as they put it. As if the most familiar acts of everyday life could be ignored! When there is no other excuse to fall back on it is asserted that we must protect the young. Today the young have seen and experienced far more than their elders. One thing is certain, we can hardly lay the blame on the young for the mess in which society finds itself.

There is much talk and anxiety today about permissiveness about the freedom to read what one pleases and do what one pleases. But if the erotic art of the masters is still regarded as filthy, degrading and demoralizing, this freedom is still suspect. It may be asked—is erotic art necessarily obscene? In literature the erotic may be couched in beautiful language, and until recently such was usually the case. To depict a man and woman in the sexual embrace in paint is another matter. In a painting of this genre one is hit between the eyes, or below the belt, if you prefer. The approach is direct, vivid, unmistakable. No beating about the bush. One sees instantly the whole works: prick and balls, cunt, teats, ass and ass-hole. It matters not whether it be a god fucking a virgin, or a drake covering a luscious nymph. In Boccaccio's time it was often the clergy who were depicted in the forbidden act, usually in a wine cellar, with a horny monk or priest tackling the maid from the rear as she decanted the wine from a huge barrel. The reproductions in this book deal only with the last three centuries, but they include so called "lewd" performances by men and women in all classes of society.

What would be a viable definition for erotic art? Whatever, I would say, excites your senses, increases your appetite, incites lust and abandon. Blaise Cendrars, the famous French writer, put it well in speaking of the *Tropic of Cancer*. "*Il y a des passages qui m'avaient fait bander,*" he wrote. (There are passages which gave me an erection.) Far from being demoralizing, I find erotic painting healthful and, for those who are inhibited or impotent, therapeutic. Psychiatrists are now recommending that such individuals seek out the erotic in art and literature as well as on the screen.

Oddly enough, the erotic works of the man whose name has become a household word, Pablo Picasso, does not seem to set with the definition given above, in my humble opinion. Free as a bird in all manner of expression, in this domain Picasso seems to pull his punches. His erotic paintings have a playful quality which adulterate the sensuality one looks for in such work. He is, of course, masterful as always and full of surprises, but his scenes are more amusing, delightful and titillating than *exciting*, in the French sense of the word. They are in strong contrast, for example, with the dead seriousness of the Japanese. If the Japanese artist does now and then lend a humorous touch to the scene by revealing in the corner of the canvas a pair of cats also going at it, there can be no mistake about the utter seriousness of the lovers. This despite the lack of expression on their faces, a lack of which is more than compensated for by the artist's concentration on the exaggerated size of the genital organs.

It is indeed a question as to what rouses us most in erotic works of art. For some it may be an excessive amount of pubic hair, for others the complete absence of hair. Sometimes it is the positions assumed by the lovers: the stand-up fuck, for example, or the woman on top of the man, weightless seemingly. Sometimes it is the expression on the woman's face, the contortion of features expressing complete abandon. Or the coupling of a satyr with a demure looking virgin or nun. Everyone has his Achilles' heel, to twist a cliché. Certainly one of the most successful methods of animating the spectator is to give the impression that he is observing the performance through a keyhole. Another is to have the couple watching themselves perform in a mirror conveniently placed above the bed. The ways and means are not countless, to be sure, but they can be amazingly ingenious and provocative. The most important thing, it goes without saying, is that the artist be an artist. Just as a good pornographic novel depends on the writer's ability to write, so it is with a painting or piece of sculpture. Even in "obscene" works of art we look for the touch of the master. The work of a hack leaves us cold or derisive. I don't say "disgusted" because, no matter how poor the work, if it sets us to thinking and hungering it has something which cannot be completely ignored.

Perhaps because of male domination, perhaps not, women have apparently contributed little or nothing in the domain of erotic art. It is only in the last half-century that we have any evidence of women producing such work, and what they have produced is negligible. It will be interesting to see, now that women are achieving "liberation," just what their approach will be and whether or not they will contribute anything new in the field of art. Will they concentrate on the male organ as men have on the female organ? Will they depict intercourse in a different manner than men have? It is hard to imagine anything new, anything startlingly different being offered us. Perhaps they will shun the erotic altogether, as being simply an expression of "male chauvinism."

If thus far women have been primarily the Muse and inspiration for men, one wonders how and what they will contribute as equals. Are they going to purify our vision or descend to the earthy level of men? It is now generally admitted that the work of the artists who created the sculptured facades of certain temples in India is the purest and highest expression of love ever attempted. In referring to these marvels of sensual love one might well say they represent the work of "liberated" individuals, of people who saw whole and gave meaning to holiness. In their work there is no division between body and spirit: all is one. No artists succeeding them have gone further. Is it fair to ask if we may expect of the liberated woman artist of the future something equivalent or better than these Indian artists have given us? The question is probably an unfair one, since liberation does not imply something better but something different. The problems we give ourselves are never resolved; at best they are dissolved.

A walk through an art museum can put one to sleep. We have had our fill of masterpieces preserved like precious mummies. When we come to erotic art we come to life. We are not interested in who painted what or when it was done; we are simply grateful to participate in the celebration of life.

Does erotic art also express Love, love with a capital L? Not always. When it does, however, when it glorifies that frail, mortal shell which is the body of man, we may well believe with the believers that man was made in the image of the Creator. In religious art the most sublime love has always glorified the body. When we take communion we partake symbolically of the flesh and blood of Christ. It's either that or we are playing at being cannibals. Myself, I experienced no ecstasy when taking my first and only communion many years ago, but I marvel every day at the wonders and the splendors of creation.

Among the more simple, natural feasts of the flesh which this body offers us is the physical union of man and woman. To it we owe not only the greatest emotional experience the flesh can know, but life itself. If the portrayal of that act, whether in words, paint or any other medium is evil, degrading and demoralizing, then those who mouth such language are sick and polluted to the core. If in ancient times it was wise and instructive to furnish the uninitiated with manuals of making love, of the art of intercourse, today it is even more important to instruct the young in the profound and mysterious meaning of love itself. For, whosoever lieth with a woman merely to gratify his sexual appetite has missed the supreme purpose and enjoyment of the act, which is to surrender one's heart and soul to the tender mercy of the beloved.

"Beauty is truth and truth beauty," wrote John Keats. The artist knows better than the priest wherein true evil lies. He is a devout worshiper and expositor of the glories of creation. He does not preach; he invites us to behold what is written in our hearts.

Henry Miller

THE 18th CENTURY

By the year 1700 the differences in artists' approach to erotic painting throughout the world were greater than their similarities. In China the base upon which sexual art rested was one in which gentle people belonging to the elite class were shown semi-clothed, engaging in stylized sex against a formal background. In Japan the base was vigorous and even violent. Sexual energy and male dominance were combined with the Japanese concept of beauty and dynamic form. In Europe the 18th century eroticism in art had come from representations of the classic sexuality in Greece and Rome, the sensuality of the Renaissance and, finally, from the repression brought on by Judeo-Christian ideas of morality.

Viewed from today's world, 18th century Europe appears to have been totally dominated by such repression, prudery and hypocrisy. Morality was defined largely by church decree, and although the prevailing rules were violated by the nobility, by the clergy and sometimes even by the Pope, painters and sculptors were faced with the stern choice of either conforming or remaining anonymous. When this period is compared with the preceding century, however, it becomes obvious that the slight cracks which had previously appeared in the walls of ignorance surrounding the arts and the sciences began to widen rather rapidly around 1700.

The great intellectual advances achieved earlier had not disturbed a comfortable conviction shared by leaders of church and state alike: that they had been divinely commissioned to interpret right and wrong for the masses of humanity. But the beginning of the 18th century brought with it skepticism, speculation, and the strugglings of a newborn tolerance. The historical accuracy of the Bible was challenged, along with the dogmas of Virgin Birth and Original Sin. Philosophers, no longer convinced that the sun orbited the earth, sought to define man's role in the universe and were joined by social critics. Notable was Voltaire (François Marie Arouet), who scathingly ridiculed the hypocrisy of both church and state. He wrote, "It is better, no doubt, to pray to God stark naked than to stain his altars and the public places with human blood," at a time when nudity was considered a more grievous sin and a more serious crime than religious or political massacre. Voltaire's acid pen brought him imprisonment, excommunication and temporary exile, it is true, but his scorn of contemporary sexual mores and censorship also acquired an ever-widening circle of intellectual support throughout Europe. Increasing tolerance, combined with an awakening awareness of human potential, was reflected in new attitudes toward both art and sex.

The depiction of sexual practices in 18th-century European art was not unprecedented. Previously, Renaissance artists had discovered that official censure did not always apply to paintings in which pagan deities were shown as gods and goddesses, who were theoretically not to be identified as real men and women. Greek and Roman mythological themes had thus become established devices for portraying naked human passions and unclothed human bodies. Similarly, the martyrdom of early

The seduction of sleeping Antiope, the Daughter of
Night, is planned by Jupiter, who has transformed himself into a muscular, masculine satyr in this symbolic
painting by Antoine Watteau. A ''painter's painter,''
Watteau was admitted to the National Academy in 1712.

Christian saints provided subject matter that allowed artists to reveal tormented bodies wracked by agony and ecstasy—the latter emotion apparently being considered permissible when it was directed toward the ethereal love of an abstract deity rather than toward the carnal love of another human's person. So a virile young St. Sebastian's nude body was shown pierced by arrows, St. Agatha displayed her severed breasts on a platter, and multiple sexual titillations temptingly surrounded St. Anthony, while Hell provided a setting for sinful but fascinating orgy.

There was nothing new in the subject matter of 18th-century erotic art. The Greeks and Romans had shown cunnilingus, fellatio, sodomy, and all the variations of heterosexual and homosexual relationships. What *was* new, in the 18th century, was the ever-increasing audience that sought sexual information through art. In previous times, guidance and counsel in sexual matters had been the domain of the physician and the priest, both of whom warned against the earthly pleasures of sexual intercourse and masturbation, which were thought to bring on insanity. Only the artist—sometimes openly, but more often anonymously—presented the joyful and ecstatic aspects of sex.

There were two levels of popular art, and the most daring paintings usually went into the private collections of nobles or merchant princes. But the invention of duplicating processes brought about an underground market in popular art. Etchings were run off in quantity in black ink and were then hand-tinted, either by the artist or by the colorists employed by publishers. In anonymous works, French, German and English artists attacked the smugness of the church, the pompousness of the military and the hypocrisy of the courts. Although popular erotic etchings portrayed sadistic and masochistic practices as well as group sex, fellatio and cunnilingus were presented only rarely. Emphasis seems to have been placed on heterosexual acts involving the nobility, in which humor—either deliberate or unconscious—was common. For example, a well-dressed lady is shown striding haughtily down a deserted lane, with a firm grasp on the exposed genital organ of a portly and equally distinguished-looking gentleman. One gets the impression that nudity was uncommon in both orgies and dalliance, and that a lifted skirt and opened trousers were considered more provocative than expanses of bare skin.

In the Orient, where the association between ancient fertility rites and erotic art had not been interrupted by the conception of Original Sin, the 18th century was also a time of change. At the beginning of the century, huge phallic images were still being carried to the rice fields of Japan when spring crops were planted, and no moral censure was involved in the portrayal of sexual acts. Erotic art was being reproduced in Japan by means of woodcuts as early as 700 A.D. Helpful manuals for lovers, complete with detailed illustrations showing positions of intercourse that ranged from the basic to the contortionistic, appeared early in the East; some, like the Hindu *Kama Sutra* (Aphorisms of Love) were ritualistic. Censorship reared its many-eyed head in China under the Mongols, who were possibly influenced by the Jesuit missionary advisers to the Emperor Ch'ienlung, during the last quarter of the century, but underground distribution of the so-called pillow books and brides' books continued in China, where they had originated, and spread to Japan in spite of official state disapproval. Throughout the Orient, the passionate paintings that depicted both the reality and the fantasy of sex were usually kept in silk-bound boxes and concealed from all save the intimate friends of the collector.

In both Asia and Europe there was interest in representations of sexuality and all the intimacies that surrounded it, but because of the dissimilarities in cultural backgrounds (as well as a lack of consistent contact between the two cultures) the spirit as well as the technique was different.

As the 18th century advanced, so did printing processes. But books were never within reach of the common man (much less the woman) in any part of the world, nor was there any way for the masses of people to view paintings suggesting that humans had sexual relations. The paintings reproduced here were the exclusive province of the rich.

Three women assault a willing victim, in "La Femme Damnée." One fondles her breast and embraces her, another kisses her breast, and the third, long dark hair streaming down, kneels between her thighs. This passionate scene, painted by the artist Tassaert, is in the Louvre Museum.

3

France

Erotic painting in the *ancien régime*, before the changes brought by the French Revolution, was deeply rooted in the earlier symbolic art of the Renaissance. Renaissance erotic art was reflected not only in the life of the nobility but in the feudal social and economic system as well. Within palaces and chateaux, symbolic erotic works graced the walls. Reworkings of passionate legends detailing rape and seduction were the popular themes. A favorite legend was the sex-charged tale of Aphrodite, Greek goddess of sex and mother of Eros, the god of love. Realistic yet romantic artists created multiple variations of nude and semi-nude scenes, with young Eros as a happy voyeur of his mother's trysts.

The classic story of Aphrodite included most of the human passions: heterosexual love, infidelity, adultery, seduction, murder and revenge. And the erotic painters of the time never tired of its diversity. After Aphrodite (always shown unclothed) married Hephaestus, she had a love affair with a young god called Ares. But she was also having an affair with the god Adonis, said to be the most handsome man in (or out of) the world. Ares, a jealous lover, on finding his mistress sexually engaged with the handsome Adonis transformed himself into a wild boar and, to the horror of the love goddess, gored Adonis to death. Later, her husband Hephaestus evened the score. He wove a huge net of bronze, trapped Aphrodite and Ares in it and displayed them atop Mt. Olympus, to the jeers and laughter of the other gods.

The story of Leda and the swan, painted by Michelangelo, was another favorite subject. It served as an excellent excuse to show the beautiful but mortal Leda in ecstasy as the god Jupiter, in the form of a giant swan, ravished her.

Early in the 18th century Antoine Watteau, then the most important painter in France, painted a lean and masculine Jupiter, who had transformed himself into a satyr, gazing lustily at the naked (but married) Antiope, whom he soon made his mistress. This was Watteau's most erotic work. It became part of the royal collection in the Louvre.

Eighteenth-century France was fortunate to have two other outstanding painters, who were responsible for some of the most erotic pictures of all time. François Boucher became *premier pientre du roi* to King Louis XV and director of the French Academy and Gobelin tapestry factories. Boucher painted intimate scenes of the king's mistresses in attitudes that were frankly erotic.

Boucher's most apt pupil was Jean Honoré Fragonard, who studied with him and became so skillful at copying Boucher's canvases that experts have had trouble distinguishing which artist painted what. It is said that when Fragonard left for the French Academy at Rome, Boucher told him that he would doubtless see the works of Raphael and Michelangelo. But, explained Boucher, should he take those painters seriously, he would be lost as an artist. It is possible that Fragonard took this advice seriously for he continued to paint and to draw in his own delicately romantic, and often erotic, style.

Fragonard worked on two levels. He painted one type of picture for the public, another type for his patrons. Drawings from his personal sketchbook, which were not meant for reproduction, showed counts and countesses engaged in sexual intercourse in luxuriously appointed bedchambers. Young girls, surprised by visitors, are revealed leaping out of bed.

One of Fragonard's most notable erotic paintings, which every school boy and girl have seen, is called "The Swing." In this seemingly innocent canvas, a beautiful girl is flying high on a swing, her skirts billowing out, while below and in front of her, her lover-voyeur reclines on the grass, looking up and under her skirts. There is no overt eroticism, but the delicate handling of this theme allows full use of the viewer's ability to fantasize. Viewers of Fragonard's time knew quite well that women did not wear underpants. They knew what the young man was seeing as he gazed upward.

Always tasteful, Fragonard became much more specific in his illustrations for the not-so-moral tales of La Fontaine. He showed counts and countesses, elaborate skirts up and satin pants down, in high-ceilinged, luxurious bedchambers making intimate love. But Fragonard's most erotic works, like those of many great 18th-century artists, were never presented for public viewing.

The effect of peeking through a keyhole at a young woman at her toilette was a favorite device used by François Boucher, the famous rococo painter. With a maid to assist her and a cat at her feet, this highborn young lady is making use of an early-day model of the French bidet.

With a long bolster pressed against her breast and clasped between her legs, this young woman seems to be lost in erotic dreams. Fragonard called the picture "Dreams of Love." In his figure painting, Fragonard was influenced by both the art of Peter Paul Rubens and that of François Boucher.

Cherub voyeurs carefully examine the nude loveliness of this well-rounded sleeping beauty. Fragonard composed his painting to draw attention to erotic content. The cherub at the right directs attention to a pink nipple, while the other two stare at her lovely golden fleece.

Fragonard, easily the most prolific erotic painter of his time, probably used his own studio as a setting for this informal sexual encounter between fully dressed members of the rich, pleasure-loving society in which he moved. His work was warm and elegantly erotic.

Three children play at sex in a barn, in this charming Fragonard memoir. The larger boy seems not to know just what to do about his erection. The girl seems to be willing to experiment, while the smaller boy appears to be giving instructions to the other two participants.

9

The French Revolution

Violent attacks on the king, the nobility, the judges and especially the army came in the form of satiric erotic drawings during the early days of the French Revolution. Drawings were often crude, always anonymous, and their purpose was to expose and ridicule the institutions that had for so long held the middle class and the peasantry of France in a state approaching feudalism. It was probably the first time that erotic painting had been organized in such a militant way. It was a reaction to the hypocrisy, the prudery and the censorship of the *ancien régime*.

Such turncoats as the Comte de Mirabeau, who tried to go along with the revolution but wanted to save the constitutional monarchy, were especially attacked. Some leaders of the church, such as Cardinal de Rohan, became the target of shockingly erotic drawings that were widely distributed throughout the new republic; Watteau, Boucher and Fragonard, with their emphasis on erotica for the elite, gave way to anonymous erotica for the masses.

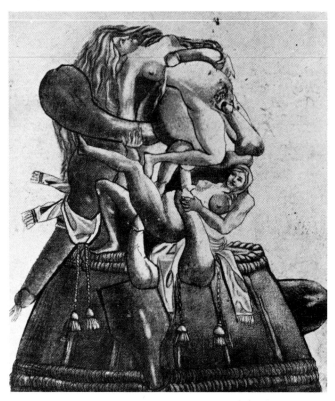

A headful of sexual fantasies makes up this caricature of the Comte de Mirabeau, which was distributed during the revolution. The caption under it read, "We must recognize that these are the noble works of the Comte."

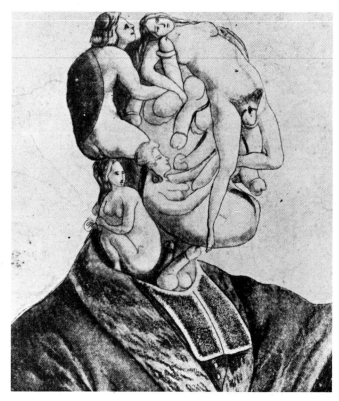

A double insult was intended in this satirical portrait of the Cardinal Rohan Soubise, for he was not only a politician but a churchman as well. The caption compared the cardinal's personality to a chill, cold wind.

This engraving satirizes the stupidity of the French military during the revolution. The woman is saying, "Oh, my friend, you are making a big mistake. Try to put the right things in the right place." Colored engravings were among the first widely distributed erotic cartoons.

It was generally known that the soldiers of Napoleon were more interested in women than in war. This caricature shows an officer being awarded a large vagina by two cherubs. Special sexual liberty for the army was the rule. Even rape was condoned during the Napoleonic period.

Before 1800 the subtle but moralistic paintings of Jean Baptiste Greuze were much admired. Here a childlike girl exposes a pink nipple, holds flowers against her pubic region and carries a pitcher. (The crack in it indicates that she has lost her virginity.) The contemporary viewer understood.

French Erotic Folk Art

Prints showing high life (and low life as well) were widely distributed in the bordellos of France. Popular steel engravings were comparatively inexpensive and were sometimes hand colored. This art lacked the elegance of the erotic art of the corrupt court, but it revealed directly and specifically the sexual pleasures of the rich and sometimes of the middle class. The poor were neglected. But sadism and masochism were shown as women birched men's bare bottoms, and men were shown birching women, although less often. Drawing-room orgies were sometimes recorded, but there was little nudity. Everyone seemed to engage in sexual pleasures fully and elegantly dressed.

The anonymous artists who produced these works led a precarious underground existence, for severe jail sentences were given out in those rare instances where the artist was brought to trial.

After the French Revolution came a period of comparative prosperity for the middle classes and a change in the type of purchaser for erotic works. No longer was such art the exclusive province of the rich and noble. And no longer did the artist depend, as he had for so long, upon the whims of royalty. The new middle class bought pictures that showed peaceful bourgeois themes. But great artists are unlikely to allow themselves to be coerced. Soon, the moral painting of Jean Baptiste Greuze gave way to Jacques Louis David's neoclassical works. Although David first painted his models nude and then clothed them, he did not produce any works that could be called truly erotic, except his large-scale "Rape of the Sabine Women," which, in spite of its strong male and female nudity and violence, was happily accepted by the French middle class and the upper class as well. David exhibited this painting in his studio for five years and collected more then 70,000 francs in admissions. Until the end of the century, he dominated French painting. There were no recognized artists (with the possible exception of Fragonard) whose works were erotic. Most reflections of human sexuality went underground until the 19th century.

Typical mulattoes of the French Caribbean islands of Guadeloupe and Martinique are pictured in this erotic vignette by an anonymous 18th-century artist. The females born of African slaves by French planters were considered passionate and attractive, and the males handsome.

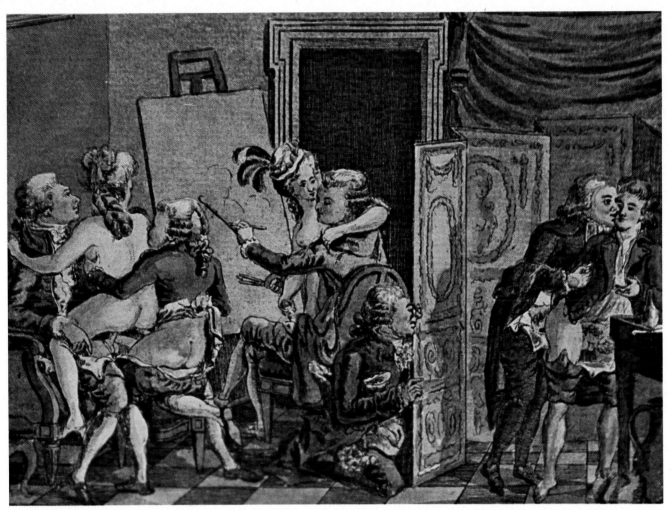

An orgy reveals some of the sexual mores of the late 18th century. A woman is having intercourse with two men, while another titillates the artist, and a voyeur secretly observes homosexuals engaged in sodomy. The French painter entitled this picture, "An Italian Artist's Studio."

Flagellation seems to have been widely practiced throughout the 18th century, as evidenced by many colored engravings and books, including numerous translations of John Cleland and the widely distributed works of the Marquis de Sade. Birch switches were preferred for whipping.

England

By the 18th century, erotic painting and drawing in England had developed on two different social levels, the highest and the lowest. Yet these two groups—the Prince Regent, earls and dukes on the one hand, the madams, whores and pimps on the other—supported considerable erotic art.

Perhaps the best-known artist was Thomas Rowlandson, a master of line drawing and of watercolor painting. Rowlandson's works were widely distributed and many hand-colored reproductions were made of them. Yet they sometimes dealt with direct nudity, and they almost always satirized the customs of the time. One of his sketches shows three whores attacking a Quaker in front of a pub. Others show lecherous old gentlemen leering at (and sometimes fondling) nubile young women.

Rowlandson became a close friend of the Prince Regent (later King George IV) and made erotic drawings for his private collection, which were far too daring to be published at that time. This valuable collection has remained largely in the hands of members of the royal family. Yet, fortunately, some of the paintings have been reproduced and are widely distributed in the underground world of erotic painting today. Rowlandson's work shows a free, easy style, a gift for the use of color and a wry insight into the sexual mores of mid-18th-century England. A number of his works are now in the permanent collection of the British Museum.

Almost equally important was William Hogarth, whose best-known etchings are "The Harlot's Progress," which is portrayed in six successive scenes, and "The Rake's Progress," a similar set of etchings. "The Harlot's Progress" tells the story in pictures of an innocent girl from the country who is taken up by a "madam." After her seduction she becomes mistress to an old man but loses him when he discovers she has a younger lover. The etchings then reveal that she becomes a thief and a whore, and by the fourth scene she has been reduced to living among pickpockets and pimps. The next etching shows her dying, after being attended by two quack doctors. We are then shown her funeral. Attending it are whores and pimps and an old procuress who is getting drunk in a corner of the room. One of the whores is picking the pocket of the undertaker.

"The Rake's Progress" was an even better known and more widely sold set of prints from Hogarth's etchings. It follows the rise and fall of a well-to-do young man through the social vices of the rich in 18th-century London. Toward the end of the 18th century Hogarth made two widely published etchings that became underground classics. One of them is titled "Before" and it shows a young woman struggling against being seduced by a portly young man. He wants her but she obviously does not want him. But in the picture called "After," he, with trousers unbuttoned and clothes awry, is trying to get dressed to leave while she, happily and gratefully, tries to make him stay. She wants him but he no longer wants her. These two drawings show that Hogarth was not always a moralist. His 18th-century citizens rarely won out against their temptations. His criticisms were directed at both the idle rich and the idle poor. Daniel Defoe, who wrote not only *Robinson Crusoe* but also one of the earliest erotic books, *The Fortunate Mistress,* said of Hogarth that only in the "middle way" did his characters find happiness.

Although illustrated editions of *The Fortunate Mistress* soon appeared, they were no competition for John Cleland's book *Memoirs of a Woman of Pleasure,* better known as *Fanny Hill.* This was the story of the sex life of a country girl, complete with detailed and vivid accounts of her loss of virginity and subsequent seductions. It was illustrated by the popular engraver Borel. Both text and illustrations provided a reasonably accurate guide to the pleasures of heterosexual intimacy for hundreds of thousands of Englishmen. The author was paid 20 guineas outright for the book, which earned millions of dollars in both illustrated and non-illustrated editions in Europe and America. It made a fortune for its original publisher, Ralph Griffiths, who earned over 10 thousand pounds directly from it.

Unlike the characters shown in sad moral tales of Hogarth and the satire of Rowlandson, *Fanny Hill* led a happy sex life and in the end was reunited with her true love.

No English artist reflected 18th-century eroticism more effectively than Thomas Rowlandson. The cheerful sexuality
of the times is recorded here as a buxom housewife gazes
tenderly at her panting lover. Once dismissed as a caricaturist, Rowlandson has since been accepted as a major artist.

(Overleaf) Sensuality is expressed not only in the position
of the lovers and the exposure of the woman, but also in the
free style that Rowlandson used in painting the swirling of
the woman's skirt and the movement of the tree branches.

17

English Erotic Folk Art

In 18th-century England, upper-class gentlemen generally had mistresses. Some of them had wives as well. But the anonymous erotic art of the time tended to show these gentlemen with mistresses and/or prostitutes. It was the day of the rake, which was a short version of the word *rakehell*—meaning a reckless, licentious "gentleman" to whom whoring and gambling was a way of life.

Before the turn of the century, Thomas Rowlandson, the great caricaturist, produced a portfolio of paintings that were later issued in book form. They showed the nobility, and occasionally even the middle classes, in the direct and lusty enjoyment of all manner of sexual activity. This now-treasured portfolio was called *Pretty Little Games for Young Ladies and Gentlemen with Pictures of Good Old English Sports and Pastimes.*

But Rowlandson was not alone. A number of artists, largely anonymous, visualized all the varieties of upper-class sexual activities. In this kind of art England did not lag behind France. A comparison of the hand-colored engravings on these pages with that of the anonymous work of French artists, shown on page 15 reveals that sadism, masochism and well-attended orgies were known in both France and England. Both of the artists have represented men as being masochists (and ejaculating), with women wielding the birch switches.

In France, although there was probably no more homosexuality than in England, there was certainly more frankness about it in the works of the erotic painters. By the latter part of the 18th century, Frenchmen (and women) had developed an unequaled reputation as a very knowledgeable people in the realm of sex. The French had also developed an enviable reputation because of the erotic works of their artists. It became de rigueur that aristrocratic young Englishmen went to Paris for their sexual initiation and education. Returning travelers from France brought home copies of the latest erotic sketches and, because a great number of Englishmen read French, they also brought back copies of the underground erotic novels published in French.

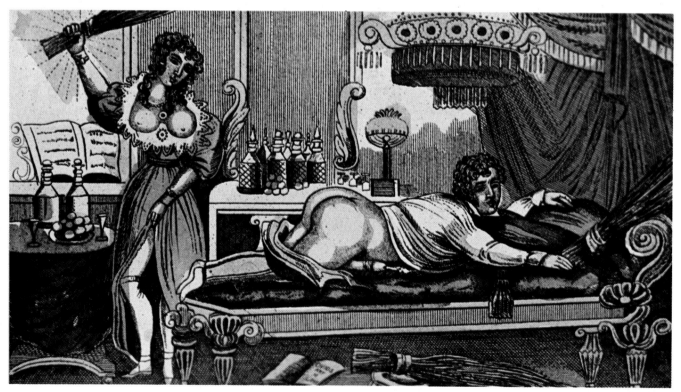

The scene is a luxurious brothel. The madam is using the standard birch switch to produce what has been called "exquisite pleasurable pain." Note the well-stocked bar, the music stand and, on the floor, extra birch switches and a copy of THE ART OF LOVE written by the Roman poet Ovid

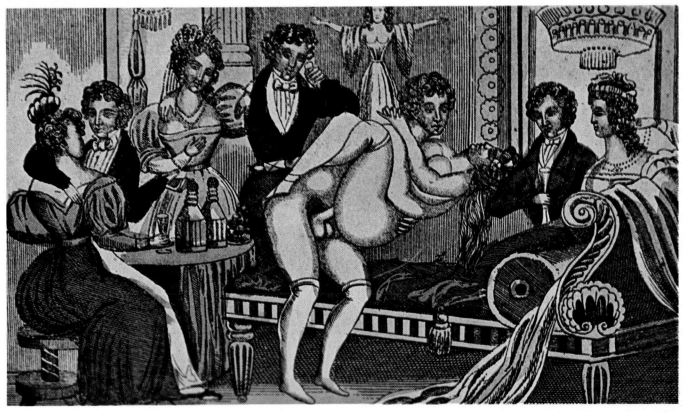

This is a private sex exhibition rather than an orgy. The setting is a high-class house of prostitution and the well-dressed women observers are expensive whores. That the artist had a sense of humor is apparent, for one patron is intently and elegantly viewing the scene through his monocle.

A rare scene within a bathhouse that seems to be part of the same expensive brothel shown above. Such luxuries as a large indoor pool had been popular in Rome but were rare in 18th-century London. The bottles indicate that the rakes of the late 18th century were hard and enthusiastic drinkers.

China

In 18th-century China the national capacity for mass organization worked against the production of all painting, erotic and otherwise. For individual freedom was not considered a virtue, and the idea that the artist should have the freedom to paint as he pleased had not yet developed. As in England, the limited amount of erotic art that was produced usually depicted royalty and was produced for them. Emperors are shown with their concubines, great lords with the women who shared their bedchambers. One other group was more rarely pictured. This was the actor class, among whom homosexuality was common (perhaps because women's roles in plays were usually taken by men). Erotic paintings sometimes showed intercourse between two men, either a young actor with a member of royalty or two actors. There were no paintings of orgies. Mass sex, unlike other mass organized activities, seems to have been unknown. Correct form, which in China was the key to success in work, seems to have extended to fornication.

Great delicacy was shown in even the most intimate bedroom scenes. There is no vigorous exertion on the part of either participant. Indeed, in one well-known painting, an emperor is seen being lifted back and forth as he sexually penetrates a supine concubine. Woman's place was an inferior one. Servants' bodies were sometimes used as pillows to elevate the buttocks of the woman whom the king was engaging. Often one concubine is shown leading the royal penis into another's inner "flower heart."

The famous novel *Jou Pu Tuan*, by Li Yü, poetically describes the three important rules to be followed by a successful mistress. First, she should lower her pleasure house for the ambassador. This means, in effect, that she should be under the man. Then to see that they have pleasure in common, she leads his *Kuei-t'ou* (tortoise head) on a butterfly chase into her *yu-kuan*, or jeweled enclosure. The third step is taken when she is on the verge of ecstasy. She requests that her lover push the head of his penis in as far as possible to reach her inner "flower heart," then to be quite still while she presses him close, as her vaginal muscles cause her "jeweled enclosure" to expand and contract so that her "flower heart" comes to rest against his "tortoise head."

According to the authors of this and other instruction books of the 18th century, the interchange of fluid at this point, and especially the warm effusion transferred directly from the female's opening to the male's *tan-t'ien*, or cinnamon stick, produces a wonderfully rejuvenating effect. Many Chinese writers recorded that, if a man can refrain from orgasm, he will receive during the woman's moments of ecstasy a vital essence, a key to health and longevity. While in 18th-century Europe the church and the medical profession were insisting upon the debilitating effects of coitus, in the Orient it was believed that the exchange of male and female fluids had the effect of recharging the human cells.

A great wave of censorship, in which many books were burned and others were expurgated, came in the last quarter of the 18th century. In 1781 the Emperor Ch'ien-lung ordered that incestuous materials and any other materials which deviated from austerity were to be removed from the imperial book collection and destroyed. Altogether the censored books numbered 2,300. Censorship went much farther than erotic books. Editors and printers paid with their lives for a line or two of poetry that might be considered treasonous.

The erotic art that *was* produced reflected the costumes and decor of the past. Costume was important, for even in the most erotic scenes Chinese men and women were rarely shown nude. Bedchambers were elaborately furnished and the artist spent as much time painting the decor, a jade vase, an ancient pottery vessel and intricately carved furniture as he did delineating the embracing figures.

A dream-like, unreal quality is inherent in Chinese erotic painting. The people seem like innocent puppets or children at play. The erotic scenes, no matter how explicit the action, have an aura of unreality almost as though sex existed on a different plane (if not a higher one) than other activities.

Interest in erotic scroll painting is greater than viewing the actual sex act, in this scene from a Chinese scroll; while two women examine the painting, another brings additional scrolls. The man and woman at the upper right, who are sexually joined, are being ignored by the rest of the crowd.

There is little curiosity on the part of court attendants as an emperor or prince takes his sexual pleasure. He appears to be engaged in sodomy with the busy attendant behind him, who is holding up the woman's leg with one hand while he directs the noble gentleman's penis with the other.

The viewing of the full moon by a group of Chinese nobles serves as a peaceful theme for this erotic painting created in the late 18th century. Even in the summer house below the viewing tower, observers take far more interest in the moon than in the royal couple that is engaged in coitus below.

24

The Chinese used sliding covers, illustrated with symbolic foliage like the flowering branches shown in upper left, to conceal erotic pictures. When the cover is pushed aside, rounded ivory figures engaged in activities similar to those here portrayed in the sensual bas-relief above are revealed.

The bursting flower at the upper right and the overripe blossom in the vase are both symbols of sex. In this painting, which derives from the Ching Dynasty, a young wife or concubine is stimulating the tip of her lover's penis with a feather, to develop his erection or to prolong its duration.

Mongolia

The tradition of the relationship of the Mongol warrior and his horse goes back to the 10th century or even earlier. By the 13th century the famed Jenghis Khan, emperor of the Mongols, with his hard-riding horsemen had triumphed over Persia and Mesopotamia, crossed the Volga, captured Moscow and Kiev, penetrated the Danube Valley and reached the Adriatic Sea. His grandson Kublai moved his horseback armies into China, which the Mongols ruled for 89 years.

Early drawings on silk showed partially clothed Mongol warriors performing acrobatic sexual maneuvers on horseback with their women. But by the beginning of the 19th century, even though the sexual acrobatics were still a part of the erotic scrolls, such drawings showed the warriors much more fully clothed. This was doubtless the result of the general moral climate, which became restrictive in the 18th century. By this time northern neighbors of the Mongols, the Manchus, had become the rulers of all China, and the Manchurian dynasties were notorious for their repression and censorship.

The horse remained a basic element in the Mongolian culture of the 18th century. It was said that a man's horses were more important to him than his wives. Mongols treated both their women and their horses well, but horses, perhaps, got the best of it. Immediate death was the penalty for horse stealing, but no such law has come down to us relating to women. And, while the use of the horse in sexual acrobatics is exaggerated in the long erotic scroll pictured here, it nonetheless indicates the importance of the animal (as important as sex itself) to these nomadic people.

The horses shown here are Mongolian ponies, some the direct descendants of the earliest modern horse, also known as the Przewalski. Having had horses perhaps longer than any other peoples in the world, it is entirely understandable that the erotic art of Mongolia would include the horses, with women as a primary image. It was said that the Mongols picked up women at one village and dropped them off at the next—having sex along the course of the journey.

In this scroll a great variety of heterosexual positions of intercourse are humorously demonstrated and, even when the acrobats are not on horseback, the horse is included as part of the artist's composition in every frame. It is probable that these drawings were made as late as the 18th century but were copies from much earlier scrolls, for the hair styles, the painting of the hills in the background and the delicate rendition of the foliage are typical of the Yüan dynasty of the late 12th and early 13th centuries. This indicates that they could have been originally drawn as early as the 13th century, for at that time, Mongol artists often painted their countrymen's nomadic life. Because they had been completely Sinicized, their painting style was Chinese. The men and women who perform as sexual gymnasts on their well-trained horses are obviously nomads, perhaps living in the then sparsely populated sections of Outer Mongolia.

Passion, excitement, joy and humor are all combined in this imaginative detail from the Mongolian scroll that is shown on the following pages. Even though the woman rides on top, the man, taking his ease stretched out along the horse's back, seems to be entirely in charge in this humorous drawing.

Japan

During the 18th century, pictures depicting the sex act were distributed more widely in Japan than in any other part of the world, partly because of the earlier invention of the wood-block print and partly because of a great demand by the growing middle class for drawings and paintings. This erotic Japanese art form flowed from a very real tradition—the celebration of sex in the springtime. The name given the art connected with these rites, *Shunga*, means "visions of spring"—spring with its fecundity, the energy of growing things, the matings of humans and of animals—this is the art called *Shunga*. In the 18th century and earlier, huge phalli were carried to the fields when the spring rice crop was planted, and the relationship between the flowing juices of nature and the lubricity of men and women is inescapable. During the ritualistic celebrations of the planting season, which were held in urban as well as rural areas, participants sometimes sought the sheltering privacy of bushes, under which they became an actual part of the flowering of spring.

No moral censure was involved in these celebrations, and the artistic depiction of sex acts was accepted and valued. It was expected that both men and women would be interested in seeing vigorous representations of the sexual act and, indeed, they were. Almost every major Japanese artist of the 17th, 18th and 19th centuries created *Shunga*.

Many of the *Shunga* drawings reflected legends recounting stories in which demons in various guises attacked women and impregnated them, perhaps while the women were engaged in such innocent activities as drawing a bucket of water or planting seeds, both symbolic acts. Animals had a place in the erotic art of Japan and were often shown copulating in a corner of a print, while a human couple participated in the same activity as the focal point of the drawing.

The depiction of legends in erotic art is not surprising, for in Japan even the legends of creation have erotic significance. A charming description of how the sexes were formed is found in an early Japanese myth. The male god, noting the differences in the female's body, asks her why she came to be that way. She explains that her body has grown normally everywhere except in one particular place, which has remained empty. The goddess in turn questions the god about his body. He replies that he, too, has grown normally except in one place—but there, *he* has grown too much. He inventively suggests that they compensate for their differential growth rates by inserting the excessive part of his body into the deficient part of hers. She accepts the logic of this solution. The motion that they made on uniting sexually is said to have been inspired by the wriggling of a tadpole upon which they gazed. (This incident may account for the many erotic drawings that show fisherfolk engaged in intercourse, while below the surface creatures of the sea are engaged in similar activity.) The legendary intercourse of these first deities caused the creation of Japan.

Shunga derived from the *Ukiyo-e*, a type of 17th-century folk art produced by a school of artists whose aim was to show the changing world (sometimes translated as the floating world) especially the daily life of the average Japanese. Life was represented realistically and erotica was part of the realism of life in all classes of Japanese society. It is generally believed that almost every great master of *Ukiyo-e* made some erotic drawings.

To the Westerner, the exaggerated size of the male organ is a striking aspect of Japanese erotic paintings, although the female vagina, too, is usually exaggerated. Yet when one realizes how the fertility symbols of the phallus and the vagina were venerated and worshipped from ancient times, it is not strange that they have more than passing importance in the art of *Shunga*. In Japan the glorification of the sexual organs never diminished, nor did the imagination of the artists depicting sexual acts.

Much has been made of the Japanese sexual instruction scrolls and books, which were often given to couples on their marriage, but these were more than mere technical manuals. They were given not only as guides to hygienic sex but also as works of art and passion, as poetic interpretations that presented the joy and fulfillment of lovemaking. Lovers treasured them, kept them carefully wrapped and put away, handled them with respect, and examined them as much for inspiration as for information.

In 18th-century Japan, wandering Buddhist nuns often played the role of prostitutes as they traveled from village to village. In this woodblock print by Isoda Koryusai, such a nun is having sexual relations with a scholar. As in many erotic prints, the couple's toes are curled to indicate ecstasy.

A new art form unique to Japan was created in the mid-18th century. It was called netsuke. The word describes miniature carvings, usually of ivory or wood, that represent the daily life, the dreams and fantasies of the Japanese people. Well-carved erotic netsuke are rare and expensive.

In this Shunga print three couples enjoy sex. The location is one of the hundreds of GAY HOUSES *in the Yoshewara district of Edo,*

むいてうらも
ちらせん

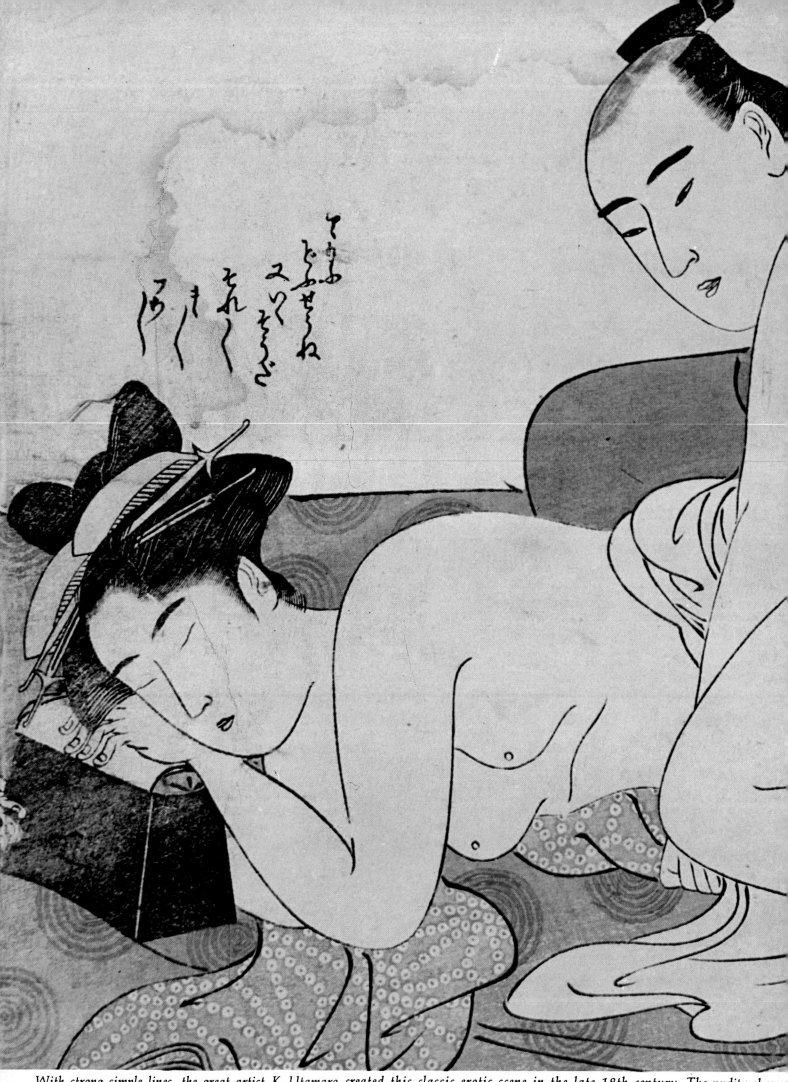

ちてあとふせんねヌりそんぢそれてきてらほ

With strong simple lines, the great artist K. Utamaro created this classic erotic scene in the late 18th century. The nudity shown

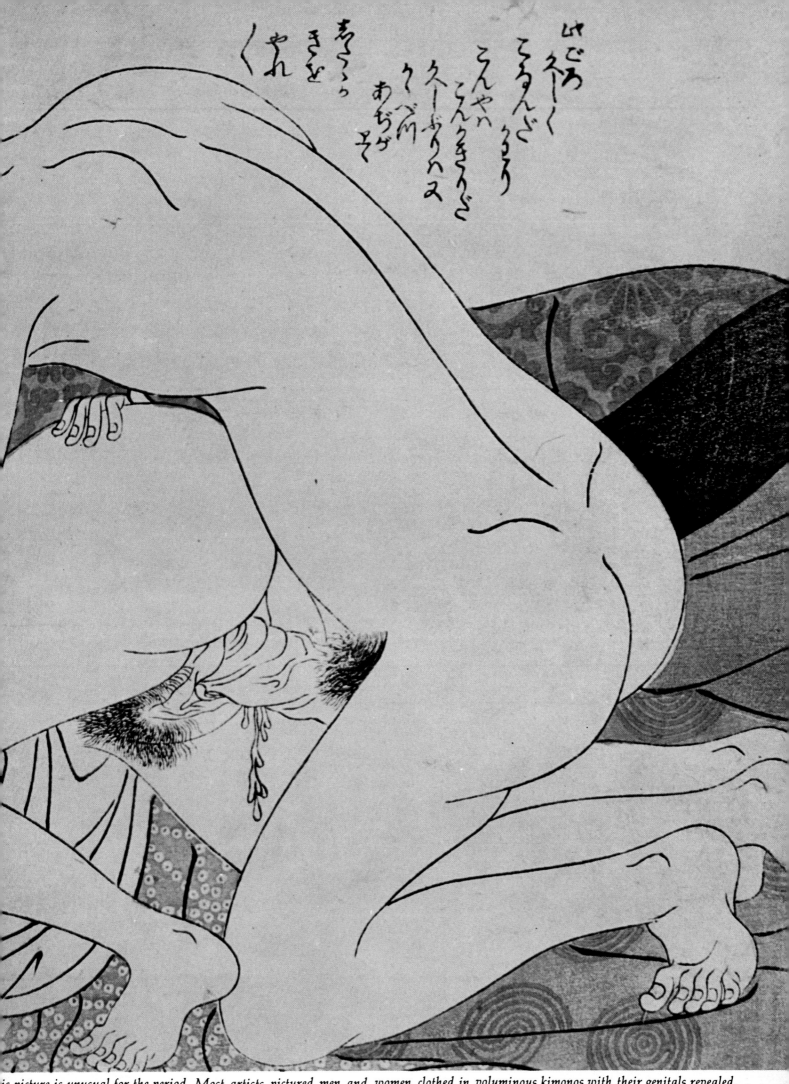

この比ろ
スしーく
てゝすんざ
ゝぎゝり
こんやへ
こんくきりざ
くーあんス
くゝぢ
あぢザ
そ

おゝろ
きゝを
やれ
く

is picture is unusual for the period. Most artists pictured men and women clothed in voluminous kimonos with their genitals revealed.

India

The gods had not become mortals in the erotic art of 18th-century India. The visualization of sexual acts was ritualistic rather than humanistic, and although the art of this period is opulent and fecund, it is almost always related to the ancient gods. It is obvious that no moral censure was involved and that drawings showing sex between deities and various females, both mortal and immortal, were permitted by the state as well as by the Hindu religion. The oral tradition relating to the sexual dalliance of the gods has been a part of Indian history and religion for 4,000 years. Heterosexual intercourse in all its forms was magnificently translated into sculpture by Indian artists from the 8th through the 14th centuries. At the great temples of Khajurāho, in the caves at Ajantā and Konārak, and at Belūr in the Deccan there are imperishable monuments to the life-giving copulation of the gods.

A revival of the Hindu religion late in the 16th century brought many of the early gods back to life, and the influence of this revival extended into the 18th century. But by this time the art of miniature painting had been brought in from Islam, and the sex life of the gods was reproduced in diminutive but exquisite detail. These paintings, formal without passion, are truly ritualistic. If love as Westerners know it is involved in the beautifully painted miniatures, it does not show. One cannot imagine the semi-nude male—pictured in his earrings, anklets, sandals, turban and transparent robe—perspiring or even moving. Nor is it possible to imagine the woman crying out in the ecstasy of passion.

This coolness, this quiet sexless cooperation, is explained by authorities on Indian religion as having to do with the tantric discipline. Basically, the principle of duality is involved—the cooperation between opposites like Zeus and Hera (Jupiter and Juno), Uranus and Gaea, yang and yin, man and woman. In India the duality is represented by the *lingam*, the male organ, and the *yoni*, the female genitals. It is explained that, like the male Chinese, the Indian is intent on prolonging intercourse and avoiding ejaculation. By the attitudes in most of the erotic paintings, it is obvious that abandoned lovemaking is avoided. Breasts are fondled, refreshing drinks are sipped, and the lingam seems permanently imbedded in the yoni (as John Updike has recently written, "with his lingam thrust into her yoni as patiently as the little Dutch boy's finger in the dike").

There is no exaggeration in the size of either lingam or yoni in Indian erotic art. But, as in the erotica of Japan and China, décor and locale are important. When the lovers are outdoors, the moon and stars are shown. When indoors, pillows and vases and the sky seen through the window are all a part of the total composition. Movement is expressed in waving palm fronds or in the brilliance of the colors used, rather than in the sexual act.

These are religious paintings. The lingam and yoni are still revered and worshipped in effigy by millions of Hindus, and the roots of this reverence go back to neolithic traditions, which became a part of oral legend and, much later, literature. A South Indian legend recounts how Vishnu—an anthropomorphic containment of the life fluid, which is all that the world consisted of at this point in time—is floating in the space of his own essence. Suddenly he sees a spectacular apparition approaching. This is Brahmā, who greets Vishnu by saying that he himself is the origin of the world. Vishnu disagrees, insisting that it is *he* who has created and destroyed the universe over and over. While the two are arguing, they perceive rising out of nothingness a towering phallus, the lingam, its tip flaming. It grows rapidly, so rapidly that they cannot begin to guess its measurements. Brahmā flies upward to reach its top, while Vishnu plunges downward. As they race on in opposite directions, neither able to see the end of the huge penis, it opens and the lord of the lingam is revealed

This exquisitely stylized gouache drawing on paper is representative of the finest art of Rājasthān India. This type of erotic art was popular at the beginning of the 19th century. In such drawings women were shown as being much smaller and as having fairer skin than that of their masculine lovers.

Intricately patterned drawings of men and women coupled in sexual intercourse that disclosed animals in motion were a favorite technique of the 18th-century northern Indian artists. These picture-puzzle designs preceded those of France, and they are dated earlier than the 18th century.

A sacred elephant is represented in this classic model of the sexual puzzle picture. Here the trunk is formed from the woman's buttocks and legs, and its tail by the long black hair of an Indian beauty. Unlike the French satires, these drawings had religious significance for those who viewed them.

as Shiva, the supreme force. Brahmā and Vishnu accept his superiority as he proclaims himself to be the origin of them all. This trinity—Brahmā the creator, Vishnu the maintainer, and Shiva the giver and taker of life—forms the base of the Hindu religion.

Philosophically, the continuing growth of the lingam is like the continuing growth of the Hindu religion, which has no limits. This immortality is often reflected in Indian erotic painting, for the very unreality, its spiritual rather than its human qualities, gives it permanence. The gods persist and will continue to exist in India's erotic art.

Almost, though not quite, the equal of the lingam is the symbol for the female vulva, the yoni, which is representative of the earth, of birth, of propagation. Like the lingam, the yoni is immortal and a goddess in its own right, and like the lingam it is a symbol of universal growth. Even in detailed paintings or huge sculptures of the yoni, the swelling that would represent the clitoris is missing, indicating that this organ had probably not yet been recognized. In one of the Indian temples there is a female figure with legs spread, exposing the vaginal lips. For hundreds of years reverent visitors have touched their fingers to their mouth and to the open cleft, until, after thousands of touches, a hole has been worn. This gesture of touching the finger to the tongue and then to the exposed vagina is a most erotic and most human gesture, which brings an intimate human touch to the cold tradition of the goddess.

There are a few paintings in which mortals are shown engaging in sexual acts with each other, but only the highest castes are represented. A rajah or maharajah is sometimes pictured with his mistress, but even then, the two are in the postures of immortals. An important exception is a painting of a rajah, seemingly affected by gynecomania, who is involved sexually with five women, his big toes burrowing into two vaginas, his index fingers in two others, and his lingam imbedded in the fifth. This has been a favorite subject of India's erotic artists.

Mortal women are presented in erotic paintings that derive from the *Rasikapriya*, a 17th-century poem by Kesava Dasa, which describes the kind of woman who dominates her lover, or who waits for an absent lover, or who is angry, or who berates her husband for being away, or who aggressively goes out looking for a lover. Women in these and other human situations described in the poem were illustrated, and by the 18th century such women had evolved into semi-goddesses called Nāyikās, who were represented as having intercourse not only with humans but with animals as well. However, these paintings of women involved in sexual acts with elephants or stallions or monkeys are not intended as realistic representations. For thousands of years the elephant has been the symbol of the great gray clouds that bring on the monsoon rains, the stallion has represented thunder and lightning, monkeys have been sacred. When women are shown copulating with these and other animals, the act is symbolic of a sacrificial act.

Another important art form is the jigsaw-puzzle type of painting, in which copulating couples form a picture of a running elephant or a running horse. These were a kind of 18th-century folk art, which also took the form of erotic paintings showing the dexterity of jugglers, balancing acts, and other gymnastic entertainment.

The contrast between complete non-motion and gymnastic gyrations during intercourse is dramatically described in the great book of Indian sexual lore, the *Kama Sutra*, which was written before the 16th century but was widely distributed in the 18th:

"When the woman holds the lingam in her yoni, draws it in, presses it, and keeps it thus in her for a long time, it is called the 'pair of tongs.'

"When, while engaged in congress, she turns around like a wheel, it is called the 'top.' This is learnt by practice only."

A most difficult balancing act is shown in this erotic folk painting from Rājasthān. Such performances actually occurred in 18th-century India; this one is probably partly true and partly humorous exaggeration. Acrobats were the leading rural entertainers of the time, throughout India.

THE 19th CENTURY

Neoclassicism faded fast during the 19th century, not only in France but also in England, Germany and Italy. In a different sense, but with the emphasis on art for the middle classes, this was also true in Japan. *Ukiyo-e* and its erotic extension *Shunga* became deeply imbedded in Japan's culture.

Throughout the world the artist was running an obstacle course, but the obstacles were being knocked over. The rising middle classes were able to buy paintings, and they showed a distinct interest in erotic works. But this evolution went on at different rates in different countries. French artists led the way, with English, Swiss and German painters not far behind. There was no erotic art worthy of the name in Russia. Japan was far in advance of China and also of India.

The world's churches, whether Christian, Mohammedan, Hebrew or Buddhist, blindly refused to accept sex as pleasure. Even in the 19th century the sexual organs were considered too repulsive to be associated with the birth of the Buddha, who was invariably shown as being born from his mother's armpit. In the Christian church there were theological attempts to promulgate the idea that not only was Christ's mother a virgin but that Mary's mother was a virgin as well, and there were even occasional attempts to explain that Christ was born through the navel of his mother or sprang from her breast. The

rigid religious wall that had been built around sex and the sexual organs was slow in crumbling. As for sex education, with the exception of some of the bride's and pillow books of Japan and China (and these had gone underground) it was only through the erotic painters that the joys of sex were visualized, and only through erotic writers that the foundations of psychology and sex education were established.

For the most part, morals and manners were split during the 19th century. There were good women and bad women. Possibly because most of the rules and the laws were made by men, this difference did not seem to extend to males. Good women were virgins until they married, and their sex relationship with their husbands was considered a duty. The morals of a woman who enjoyed sex with her husband were suspect—as property, she was expected merely to submit. This attitude, world-wide in the early 19th century, began to erode only in France and England. With sexual pleasure denied and masturbation considered a sin (and an unhealthy one at that), a moral and sexual revolution had to be the ultimate result.

Fortunately, avant-garde writers and painters surreptitiously as well as openly began to fill the need for a pleasurable approach to sex. Religious leaders had pushed humanity so far in restricting pleasure that both women and men wore long night-

Parisians wanted to know what had been going on at this picnic in a Paris park painted by Édouard Manet and titled "Le Déjeuner sur l'Herbe." Critics saw many erotic symbols, including the walking stick, the spilled fruit, the position of the bathing girl's left hand and the man's extended finger.

gowns—and one style of nightdress even had a hole in the front, allowing intercourse without bodily contact except directly with the genitalia. Sex was kept in the dark in many ways. Some husbands and wives never saw each other naked during their entire marriage. It is no wonder that the reaction against this puritanism brought paintings of nude men and women that showed the charm of sinfulness, that promoted sex as pleasure. Artists like Degas showed prostitution, Félicien Rops depicted masturbation, Jean François Millet portrayed sex in the outdoors and, as is shown on these pages, most of the great painters of the time celebrated the joys of sex.

Social evolution, like biological evolution, sometimes involves sudden change but more often comes about gradually. In the 19th century the slow change from erotic painting based on symbolism to that involving more realistic attitudes finally became pronounced. It was not an immediate turnabout but rather a wearing away of the old attitudes that had depended upon subterfuge by portraying mythological figures or religious symbolism. The permanent themes in erotic painting that crossed all lines of nationalism, philosophy and geography continued to be affection, love and sex. But as sex continued as a creative source for painters, the success of the French and American revolutions opened up a new view of the importance and dignity of modern man and brought about distinct changes in the visual arts. For the first time specific sexual acts involving normal men and women appeared as paintings, etchings and watercolors. They were by recognized artists and were exposed to public viewing.

It must be remembered that the artist did not (and does not) think of himself as a teacher, but as a sensitive recorder and reproducer of life in his era. Some painters continued to depict historical and religious events in the 19th century, but a new wave of erotica, showing life and love, also began to appear.

These, then, were dilatory evolutionary changes. An abrupt change in erotic art also came, with the introduction of women's drawers. Women were slow to adopt them at first, but by 1825 drawers were generally worn by the upper class, the middle class and many of the peasants in Europe. There is no question but that the advent of drawers was responsible for great changes in style and in the status of women. Skirts began to rise slowly, almost imperceptibly. There was still an obsession with layer after layer of clothing. The church, the doctors, the stylists all saw to that. The flesh-and-blood woman vanished. Even prostitutes charged extra for taking off their clothing, partly because of the trouble involved and partly because nudity was generally considered a perversion. This conspiracy to hide the female body was world-wide. The kimono and the obi became more bulky in Japan. Chinese women wore so many layers of clothing that it was impossible to tell what they looked like. And as for Europe, there were corsets and endless underskirts and, in addition, veils, hats and gloves. Even though drawers were almost universally worn, they were never mentioned and, in fact, were generally known in English-speaking countries as "unmentionables."

Only the artist was interested in bringing back the woman who was hidden under the disguise of fashion. Only the artist seemed to see the beauty beneath. Neither artists nor models were respectable, yet the repressed 19th-century man and woman could not but envy their physical and moral freedom.

By mid-century drawers became visible, with the introduction of a dance that might be considered the most sexually liberating influence of the 19th century in Europe. This was the cancan. Not only were drawers flaunted, but it could now be clearly seen that women had two legs and that they were capable of moving them in many attractive ways. Toulouse-Lautrec not only celebrated the cancan in his widely distributed posters, but he was among the first of the 19th-century artists to create compassionate paintings of prostitutes and lesbians.

The painters were not alone in their attractive portrayals of the ways of prostitutes. Indeed, from the middle to the end of the 19th century prostitutes were sympathetically portrayed by Emile Zola in *Nana,* by Alexandre Dumas fils in *La Dame Aux Camélias,* and in Guy de Maupassant's *Bordel de Madam Tellier*—works that were instantly popular.

The relationship of the blonde head of the man to the hips and belly of the woman gives erotic emphasis to this allegorical painting by Chassériau. Such intimacy was acceptable because the man represents Apollo and the woman Daphne, the wood nymph who transformed herself into a laurel tree.

Europe

In 19th-century Europe there was a continuous increase in the quality, the quantity and the acceptance of erotic painting. Yet from 1800 to 1900 the tides of human enlightenment ebbed and flowed. Although the French Revolution influenced sexual liberty in Switzerland, Germany and—to a lesser extent—Italy and Spain, by 1815 reaction had set in. Russia, Prussia and Austria formed the Holy Alliance, in an effort to combat the increasing demand for individual human rights. Even more repressive was the Quintuple Alliance, in which these nations were joined by England and France in a union that sought to preserve royal privileges and to reestablish absolute control over the common man and woman. Although divorce had become legal in France as a result of the revolution, it was abolished. England became increasingly conservative under William IV, and by the beginning of Queen Victoria's long reign no divorced person—English or foreign—was admitted to Buckingham Palace. The works of Shakespeare and Chaucer were expurgated, and Defoe's *Robinson Crusoe* and *The Fortunate Mistress* were adjudged obscene. Certain passages of the Bible came under serious criticism.

It would seem that sexual enlightenment may be a corollary of censorship and repression, for out of the early 19th century came some of the most erotic and satiric works of art of all time. One of the tradition-breakers was Honoré Daumier, born in 1808. Because of his penetrating visual disclosures, Daumier's erotic paintings have a shocking effect. He mirrors the human condition not glamorously nor romantically, but with deep compassion and sharp insight.

Some of the finest erotic impressions appear in the sketchbooks of Jean Auguste Dominique Ingres that were discovered after his death. Had these intimate drawings been revealed during his life—while he was a director of the French Academy, a member of the French legislative body and an officer in the Légion d'Honneur—his career would have been ruined.

The distribution of colored etchings and lithographs dealing with erotic subjects moved rapidly through Europe. A steady improvement in printing processes and in communication between nations contributed to their spread and an ever-increasing audience of art-hungry students began to demand erotic art, as did a rising merchant class that was willing to pay well for paintings.

The fleshy works of Antoine Wiertz were popular in Belgium and Germany, and the erotic drawings of Michael von Zichy were known to students and connoisseurs from Berlin to Leningrad. But the greatest examples of erotic art flowed from France. Gustave Courbet used no screening legends, no diaphanous drapery to conceal his powerful sexual images. The art world was electrified by his painting "The Sleep," which shows two nude women with legs and arms erotically entwined. Today, viewers still flock to see it at Musée du Petit Palais in Paris. But Courbet's "Woman's Torso," with a graphic and almost life-sized vagina in the foreground, is not publicly exhibited even now.

Previous concepts of permissible erotic subjects were completely overturned by the impressionist Édouard Manet, in his instantly famous "Le Déjeuner sur l'Herbe" ("Lunch on the Grass"). In this painting, a naked woman sits with two fully dressed men while another woman, semi-clothed, bathes in the background. Originally titled "The Bath," this painting was angrily rejected by the Paris World Exposition of 1855. But Napoleon III, who prided himself on his modern views, intervened and ordered that it be exhibited. Conservatives and traditionalists were shocked. They would have been even more alarmed had they known that their reigning favorite, Franz Xaver Winterhalter (who had painted Queen Victoria) would soon portray a young lady sans drawers crossing a brook, her vagina and pubic hair clearly reflected in the water.

Toward the end of the century, the writings of Leopold von Sacher-Masoch influenced not only literature but also art. The theme of his works usually

---

Eroticism abounds in this detail from the famous Ingres painting "Le Bain Turc," painted in the year 1862. Lesbianism among the inhabitants of the Turkish harem is realistically shown, and only the classical allusion to a foreign culture made it possible to exhibit this painting in public.

involved dominant, cruel women and the men who enjoyed being punished by them. In his most important novel, *Venus in Pelz (Venus in Furs)*, the heroine binds her lover and beats him to the point of orgasm. There had been erotic paintings illustrating this theme before Sacher-Masoch, and his works had no great literary quality. Yet he brought into focus the principle of pleasure from punishment and, as the word *sadism* derived from the earlier works of the Marquis de Sade, the word *masochism* derived from the works of Sacher-Masoch.

Despite the cyclic repressions of human sexual liberty that occurred during the 19th century, there was a slow and continuous movement in the direction of more realistic, open attitudes toward sexual enjoyment. Out of each repressive cycle, the works of talented and liberal artists and writers survive—to educate and entertain later generations.

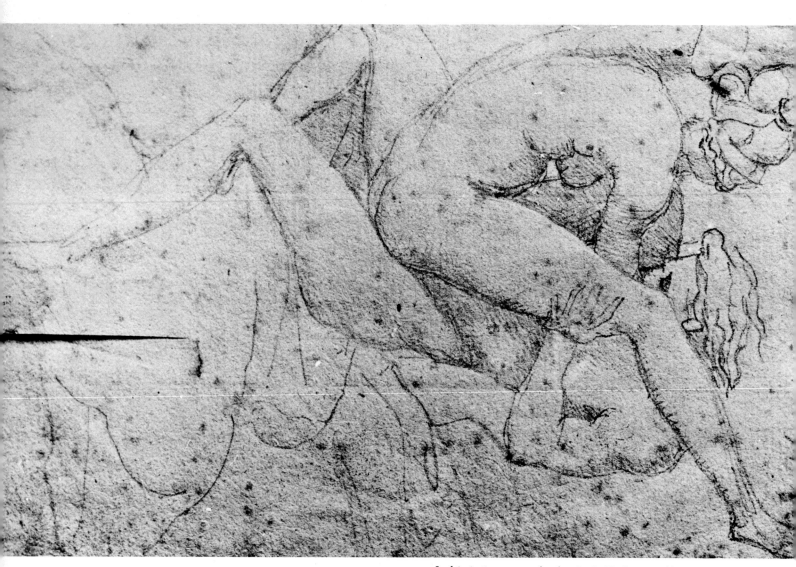

In his intimate notebooks, J. A. D. Ingres allowed his imagination complete erotic freedom. Yet even in these most intimate sketches, although his line technique is freer than in his painting, the participants in sexual intercourse still retain the classical appearance of legendary god and goddesses.

The goddess Leda is seen in the ecstasy of orgasm, as she enjoys sexual penetration by the god Zeus in the form of an enormous swan. Although many great artists, including Michelangelo, have used this theme, none has shown the unique coupling of goddess and bird with such intensity

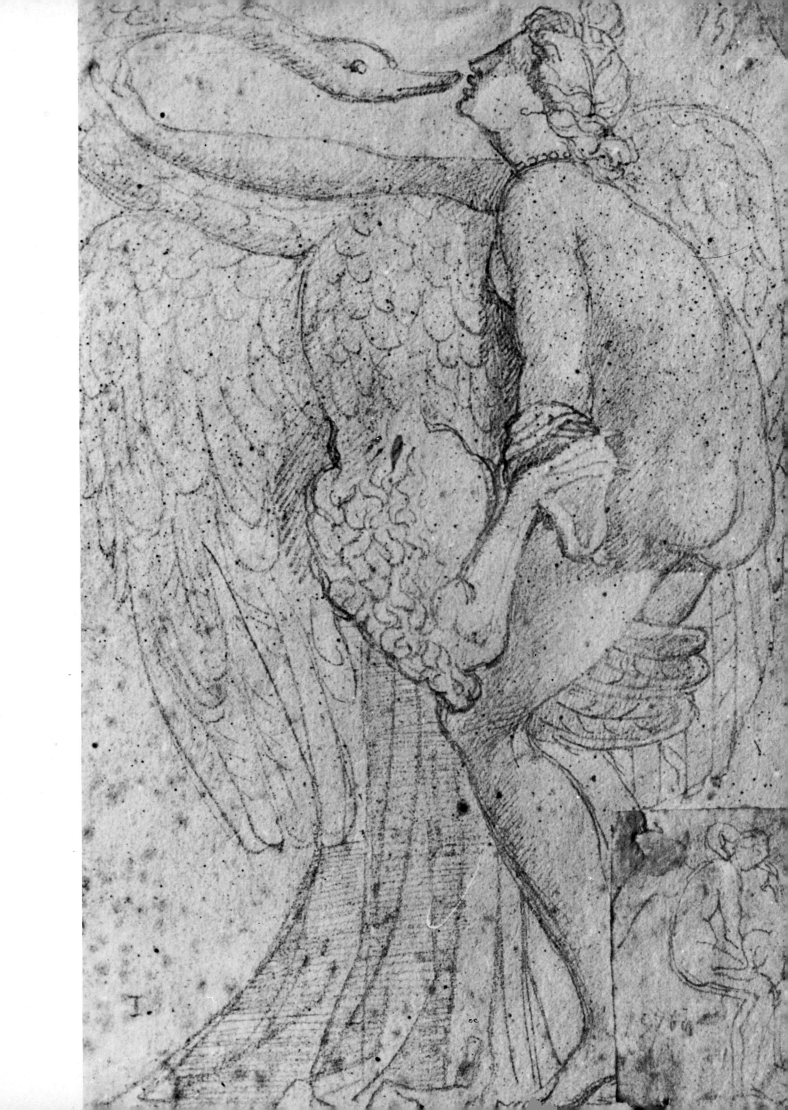

After escaping from Venus, his over-protective mother, the precocious love god Cupid enjoys sex with his true love, the beautiful maiden Psyche. In this and other long-hidden pen-and-ink sketches discovered in his notebooks, the artist Ingres found an outlet for the release of his own hidden sensuality.

The great German art critic Ernst Fuchs considered this watercolor and the one on the following pages to be among the finest works that Honoré Daumier had ever created. Fuchs said, "Everything that makes Daumier great culminates in them. Every stroke is the most genuine Daumier." These two great examples of the painter's erotic works were dedicated to his good friend Louise in the month of April, 1863. Her name can be seen in the lower left-hand corner of the overleaf painting. Although their existence has been known for many years, these two paintings have never been reproduced before.

53

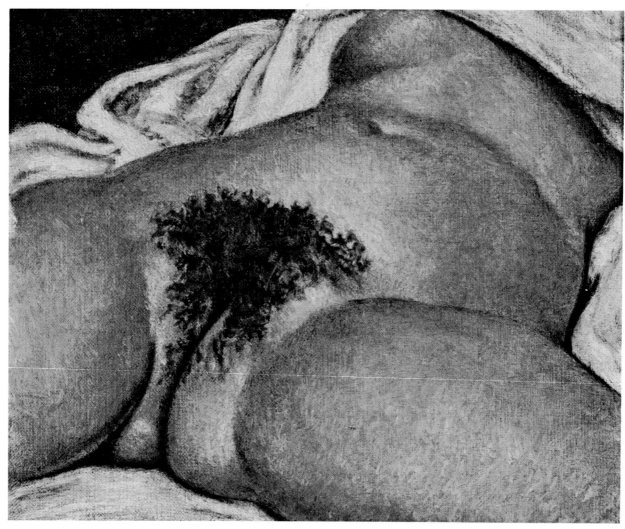

The ultimate in erotic realism was reached by the great master Gustave Courbet in this painting, which he called "Woman's Torso." The roundness of the body, even the texture and warmth of the flesh, is vividly painted. Never publicly displayed, the painting has been seen by very few people.

Woman-to-woman sexual relations have always been more visually acceptable than those between men. In this sensuous painting by Courbet, both figures are erotically exciting—note especially the extended nipples of the breast. First called "The Sleep," this work is also known as "The Friends."

In these two sentimental and poetic scenes, Charles Édouard de Beaumont shows the tenderness and wonder of a man and woman exploring one another sexually. Although other de Beaumont paintings have been widely exhibited, these two works have been in private collections for nearly a century.

It will come as a surpirse to the many admirers of Edgar Degas, who know him only for his painting of innocent and dedicated ballet dancers, that he was also the painter of a considerable number of erotic works. Yet he visited both the simple and ornate bordellos of Paris and produced both aquatints and monotypes (engravings) showing madames and whores at work and play. Unlike Toulouse-Lautrec, Degas held himself aloof from the underworld life of Paris. His paintings in this genre were influenced by a short story by Guy de Maupassant, MADAME TELLIER'S BROTHEL, which, with Degas' illustrations, became a much sought-after erotic book. The ribald story recounts the adventures of a famous madame and her girls when they take a holiday in the country. The climax comes when they return and give a sentimental party for their lonely gentlemen clients.

(Above) Four relaxed whores wait for customers in this monotype (a form of etching) made by Edgar Degas. (Below) A happy voyeur-client gazes with delight as one of the girls pins up her long hair in preparation for her bath. Many of Edgar Degas's most sensuous paintings are of women bathing.

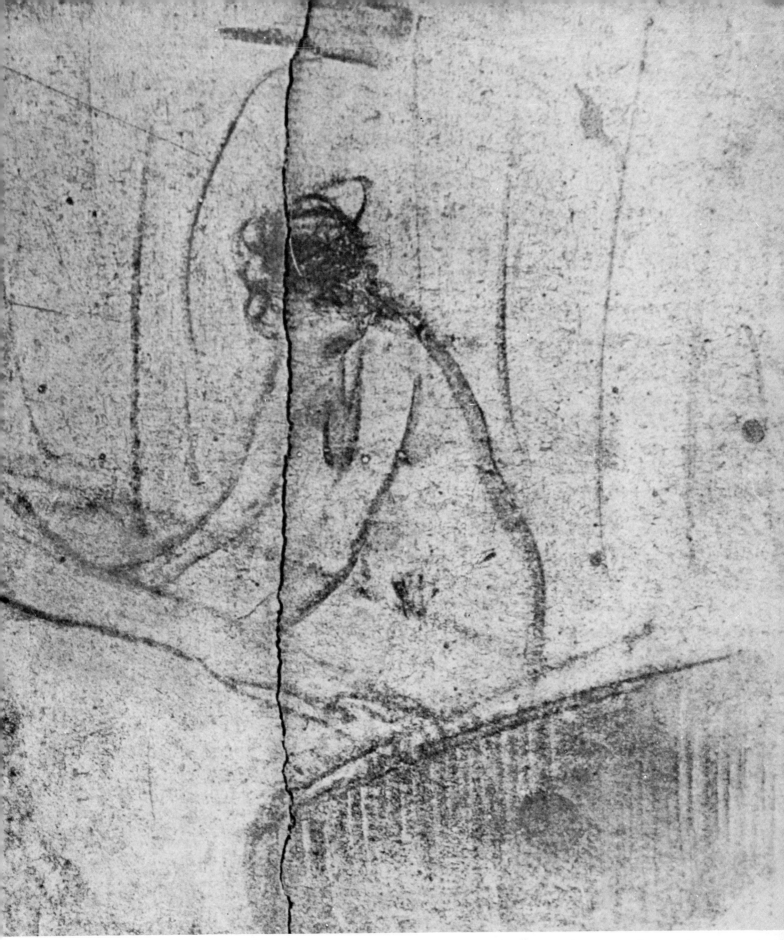

In this monotype by Degas, never before printed, a prostitute lying on her stomach fellates a fat client. On the right another whore, entirely nude, seems to be massaging the leg of the girl. The plate was broken in half and discarded, quite probably because Degas did not think it was worth printing.

All techniques of drawing and painting interested Henri de Toulouse-Lautrec. In the rare pen-and-ink sketch (above), an ailing penis allows itself to be comforted by a high-breasted young woman with a cup of tea or coffee. Lautrec throughout his adult life had a great interest in erotic themes, many of which he treated humorously or satirically. Because he lived in the country, Toulouse-Lautrec doubtless observed the mating of many different animals. In the amusing sketch (below), his keen eye and facile hand produced a minor masterpiece of sexual intercourse in a French barnyard between two pigs.

With strong, simple lines and harsh colors, Toulouse-Lautrec shows a Parisian prostitute putting on her stockings while her friend waits. Lautrec seems to have seen the world through the eyes of a cynic. Yet he painted women of society, of the theater and of the bordellos with sensitive insight.

Eroticism was expressed in many of the paintings of Paul Gauguin, but never so specifically as in this small sketch of Tahitian natives sexually joined. It was not exhibited until many many years later and then rarely. Gauguin also made at least one woodblock showing Tahitians similarly engaged.

Portrayer of kings and queens, Franz Xaver Winterhalter was a popular conservative artist. But upon his death it was found that he had left a locked trunk containing a series of large erotic canvases. One was "The Treacherous Water Reflection," a portrait of Lola Montez, mistress of King Ludwig.

The Devils and the flesh

During the 1830s an ingenious artist, Eugéne Le Poitevin, found a way to produce erotic pictures and to blame their eroticism on the devil. A series of lithographs called *Les Diableries Erotiques* appeared, hand-colored by the artist. In these prints the devils played many pranks, usually on innocent-looking females. The etchings were sometimes satiric, sometimes violent, but were usually highly amusing. They are, in fact, the most amusing series of erotic drawings to have appeared up to 1830.

The humor was usually that of exaggeration. In one picture two young girls go to the fair and pay to look through a peephole, where they see the erect penis of a devil. In another a blind Cupid rides a huge penis, which in turn has its own penis. Penises and vaginas fly through the air like butterflies, are gathered in baskets and, personified, play games with adults and children.

Imitations of the Le Poitevin originals were widely copied and sold as individual prints, and were even collected into books. The color reproductions shown on these pages are from the first of the original hand-colored books. The sense of fantasy and the bizarre imagination of the artist are reminiscent of the style of the 16th-century Dutch painter Hieronymous Bosch.

A young woman uses the extended penis of a helpful devil to water her garden. One potted plant appears to be distinctly phallic. By supplying the devil with a large vase to drink from, the artist implies a continuous flow from this uplifted reservoir to the most convenient garden hose.

A diabolical game of leapfrog on the banks of a stream concludes with Lilliputian demons diving headlong into the vulva of a partly submerged human female. In the far right-hand corner the inventive artist has painted a froglike penis that appears to be squirting a stream of liquid material.

An ingenious battering ram, with a detached penis and testicles, has been devised by the devils to deflower a determined and cooperative virgin. The prevailing view was that all sex was evil—so if such ideas were to be visualized, then the devils could reasonably be held responsible for them.

Famous for such quietly religious canvases as "The Angelus" and "The Man with the Hoe," Jean François Millet was one of the most contradictory of all 19th-century artists. Although he sometimes used erotic themes, these works were completely unknown outside his most intimate circle. The public, faced with Millet's erotic art, would find it hard to believe that the same artist was responsible for the pious canvases. Yet this painting of a couple having coitus in the fields shows the same respect for bucolic bliss and human sentiment that is evident in Millet's conventional works.

In this Millet painting, a woman in a deep crouching position fellates the devil. From the viewpoint of the artist, this may have been a moral painting, with the devil representing temptation. As late as Millet's time, it was believed that on the Sabbath, witches had to kiss the ass of the devil.

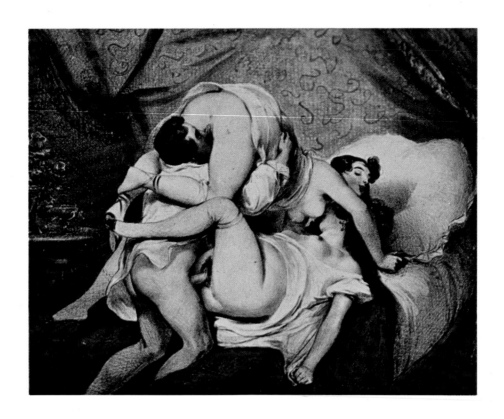

These three sex-saturated scenes were painted in the mid-19th century by Achille Devéria, who was the recognized master of the most specific erotic drawings of the period. Above are two illustrations for a private edition of DON JUAN. At right is one of his favorite themes—the harem.

The theme of women having intercourse with animals goes back as far as the early rock drawings of Africa. In this 19th-century example, Devéria has exaggerated to the point of making the sex act with the donkey ridiculous. In the picture on the right, his imagination has also run away with his sense of reality or proportion, as a woman with huge buttocks attempts intercourse with an ape-man who could not even have existed in a circus sideshow. Devéria's illustrations were widely distributed in privately printed editions of the erotic novel GAMIANI, written by Alfred de Musset.

As a watercolorist, artist Constantin Guys has been compared with his colleague Daumier. Most of Guys' paintings depict horses, the military and women. But it was women, and his emphasis of their sexuality, that made him famous. In his drawings, female genitalia are exaggerated.

Aubrey Beardsley, master of the black-and-white pen-and-ink drawing, became extremely popular in both France and England during the late 19th century. Unlike Constantin Guys, Beardsley exaggerated the penis rather than the vagina. His semi-erotic works have been widely distributed.

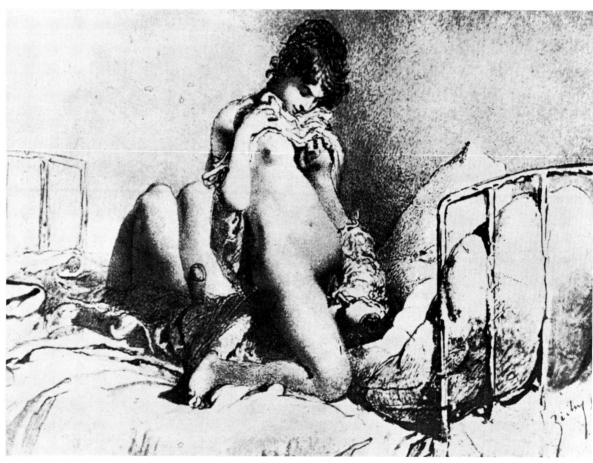

An almost unknown master of erotic painting was Michael von Zichy. Von Zichy could and did show men and women realistically in a great variety of sexual situations, yet the paintings were never vulgar. One of his sketches (right), shows penises being tickled, fondled and masturbated.

A special flavor of eroticism pervades the women painted by Renoir. He was obsessed by their curves and loved to paint the texture and warmth of their skin. Renoir's paintings are so deeply infused with passion that he has been quoted as remarking, "A good picture must be painted with the prick."

The end of the 19th century and the beginning of the 20th can be marked by the works of Renoir, who was nearing the end of his creative period, and those of Pablo Picasso, who was beginning. Picasso's paintings date from the end of the 19th century. He painted at least three erotic works before 1900.

Asia

Erotic acts are visualized against the social evolution of society. The society's attitudes toward sex and sexual art cannot be separated from its total culture. Nineteenth-century China and Japan are classic examples of how the different sexual values of two Asiatic societies were reflected in the erotic works of their artists. In China individuality had been and continued to be discouraged, the nonconformist was almost nonexistent; the family group, village group, national group was everything. It follows that there was no climate for the growth of the kind of talent that creates great erotic art. While Europe was producing a wave of strong-willed, radical, unique artists and writers, the Chinese artists were content to copy earlier erotic pictures.

The new spirit of investigation pushed on in Europe as scientists set out to describe as completely and as exactly as possible the variety of life in all its forms and shapes, and painters set themselves the task of showing completely and exactly the sexual ways of humans. Yet Chinese society continued to submerge personality and to produce no erotic masterpieces and little erotic folk art. Unlike France, Germany, England and the Netherlands, the 19th-century Chinese neither studied sex nor did they illustrate it. Instead they decorated it. The ultimate result was that sexual relations were shown behind a wall of caste and custom. Erotic paintings showed a static interplay of small penises and delicately drawn vaginas, against a formal background of ancient feudal court life. Only the Chinese sense of humor occasionally lifted these works out of banality. In some of the outdoor pictures there is a spirit of playfulness with even the breeze playing a part in the gentle sexual encounter.

Considering the Chinese society's concentration on other than sexual aspects of life, it is interesting that at least a minimal amount of traditional erotic art, even though it was of poor quality, continued to be produced. It indicated that socially, morally and ...ie' lly the Chinese civilization had not been affe...d by ... ,estern thought and customs that had

been introduced in China before the mid-century. The scientific, economic, political and sexual ways of the West were not assimilated. Public kissing and displays of affection seen in Western book illustrations and drawings had no noticeable impact on Chinese erotic painting. A few paintings showing Chinese women with Western men were attempted, but the artistic level was primitive at best. Even the delicate naïve gentleness achieved by 17th- and 18th-century painters was lacking. Colors became garish, anatomy angular, and in many examples (even those painted as late as 1870 and showing Western influence) women were still depicted with bound feet.

In India, as in China, important erotic painting came to a dead stop in the 19th century. Earlier motifs were repeated, earlier legends continued to be illustrated; and this was to be expected for no great individual artist emerged. The old gods of India had gone underground; new ones remain to be created.

The Japanese viewed the 19th-century world differently. They reached out for all the scientific methodology that the West offered. There were far-reaching and continuous changes in economics, politics and art—especially erotic art. The 18th century had left a distinguished heritage. Both the people's art, called *Ukiyo-e*, and the erotic art of *Shunga* had become highly regarded. The master of both forms, Kitagawa Utamaro, produced some of his finest works toward the end of the 18th century and continued to paint masterpieces until his death early in the 19th century.

Unlike the Chinese, the Japanese had long before dispensed with the polite, formal and understated erotic themes. In the works of Utamaro and Eisen men and women came together like thunder and lightning. The size of the sex organs grew until they seemed to fill the picture. By mid-century such artists as Eisen, Kiyonaga and Kuniyoshi and a new master, Hokusai, were well established as painters of erotic subjects. The great tradition of *Shunga* painting died with the deaths of these artists.

Nudity was rarely pictured in the erotic art of China, and anatomical details were obviously not considered important by the painter of this work, who preferred to concentrate his efforts on the headrest block, on the design of the rug beneath the couple, and on the background of flowers and delicate leaves.

A unique erotic painting from 19th-century China uses exaggeration to make its humorous point—that not even travel should interfere with sexual pleasure. This is a rare example of erotic humor. In most Chinese erotica of this period the humor is subdued, and the scene is more likely to be domestic.

This illustration and the one on the following page are from
A BOOK OF SPRING PAINTINGS. Books such as these, called
''pillow books,'' were presented to newlyweds. The size and
features of the participants indicate that these paintings came
from Mongolia. The time: end of the Ch'ing (Manchu) Dynasty.

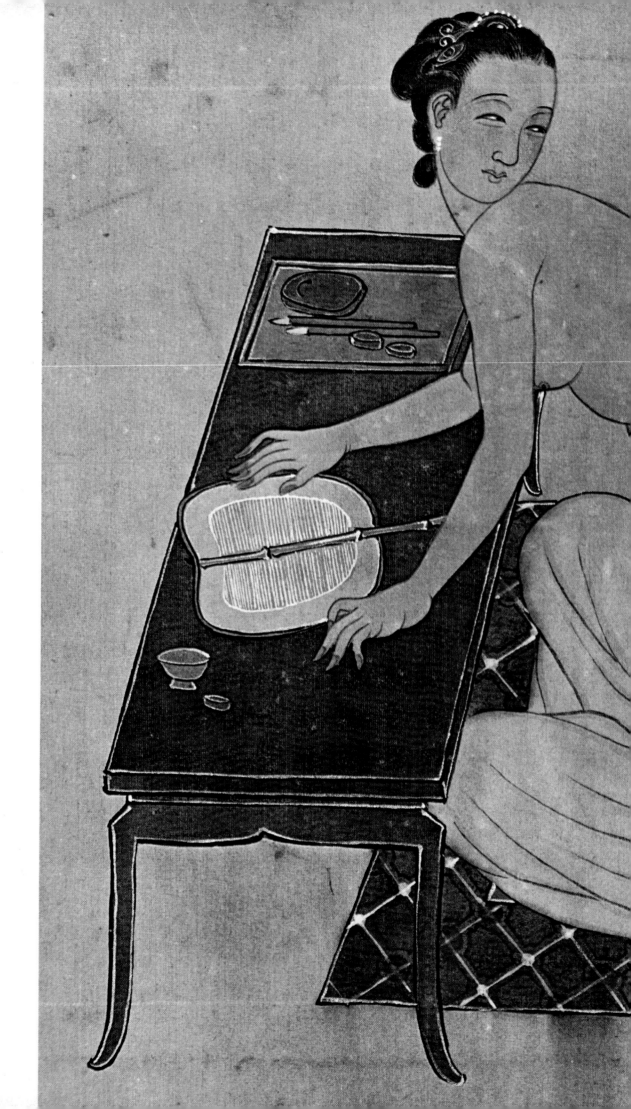

This charming rendering has the same mild humor and naïve approach found in the great majority of Chinese erotic works. The voyeur theme is also a common one in China. In a high percentage of erotic works some person, unseen by the characters in the painting, observes them.

Based upon a considerable number of examples, group sex among the aristocracy was not unusual in 19th-century China. Each feudal lord had a large complement of concubines in addition to his wives. Indeed, it is characteristic of group sex paintings that women usually outnumber men.

(Overleaf) The swing is one of the themes in erotica from the Orient. Little or no attention is given to anatomical detail—the overall scenic effect seems to be of prime importance. In this woodland setting the young woman is being moved gently up and down by her friend who pulls the tree branch.

One of these two scenes, created by Utamaro, compares love-making to a journey. The woman, who wants to continue, says, "We are only part way home." The man wants to stop and rest, for he is nearing the end of his journey. But the woman says, "Let's not stop yet—let's go on to the corner."

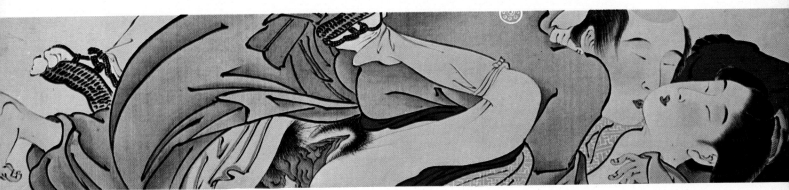

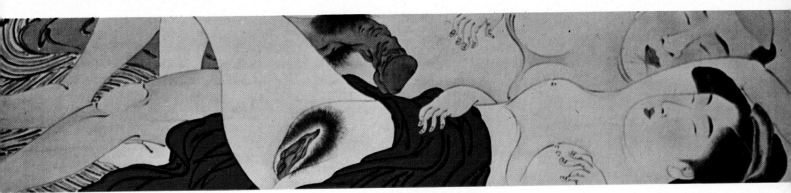

A long narrow scroll of the late 19th century shows a se-
quence of a Japanese couple's lovemaking. In the first panel
the man is wetting his fingers with his lips. The woman
seems apprehensive. In the second panel the orgasm has been
reached. (Note curled toes.) In the third both are relaxed.

Lesbians are preparing to use a dildo for their lovemaking in this detail from a famous Shunga painting. One of them is offering the other a sr

ainer of ointment and saying "Put this on the dildo or it will not go in easily." The other says, "Hurry, for I want to have many orgasms."

In a detail from one of the great Shunga paintings the artist has conveyed extreme motion with a great economy of line. The swirling lines of b...

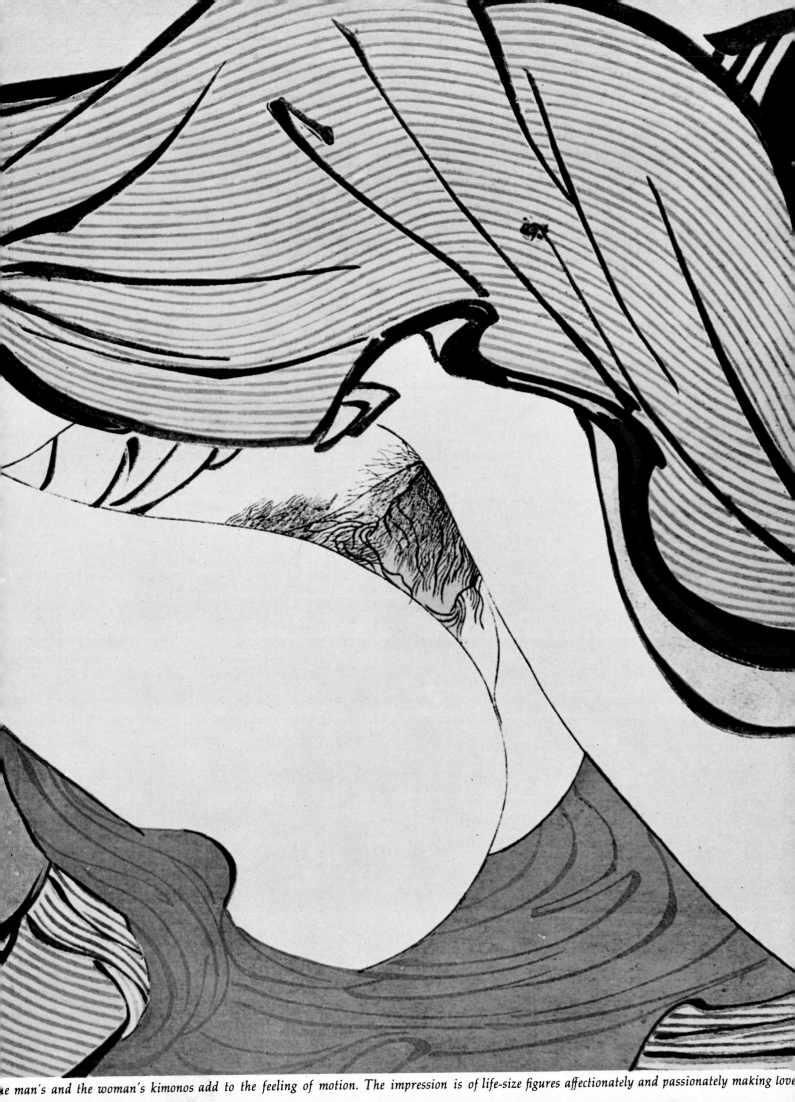

e man's and the woman's kimonos add to the feeling of motion. The impression is of life-size figures affectionately and passionately making love

Last of the great Japanese painters in the UKIYO-E tradition was Katsushika Hokusai, who died in the mid-19th century. This erotic woodblock print is intricately detailed to show the design and texture of the kimonos and the passion of the geisha who is tenderly holding her lover against her breast.

A classic example of Persian erotica includes candelabra and food dishes at the very bottom of the painting. The two lovers are clothed only in jeweled anklets, necklaces, earrings and sandals. The scene is on the terrace of an Arabian Nights-like palace with an overlooking crescent moon.

In a humorous painting a Persian warrior is having sexual relations with a seemingly pleased donkey. Yet for safety he has put his scarf around the donkey's forelegs and carefully holds the back legs together. Although the warrior's weapons are of an earlier period, the style is 19th century.

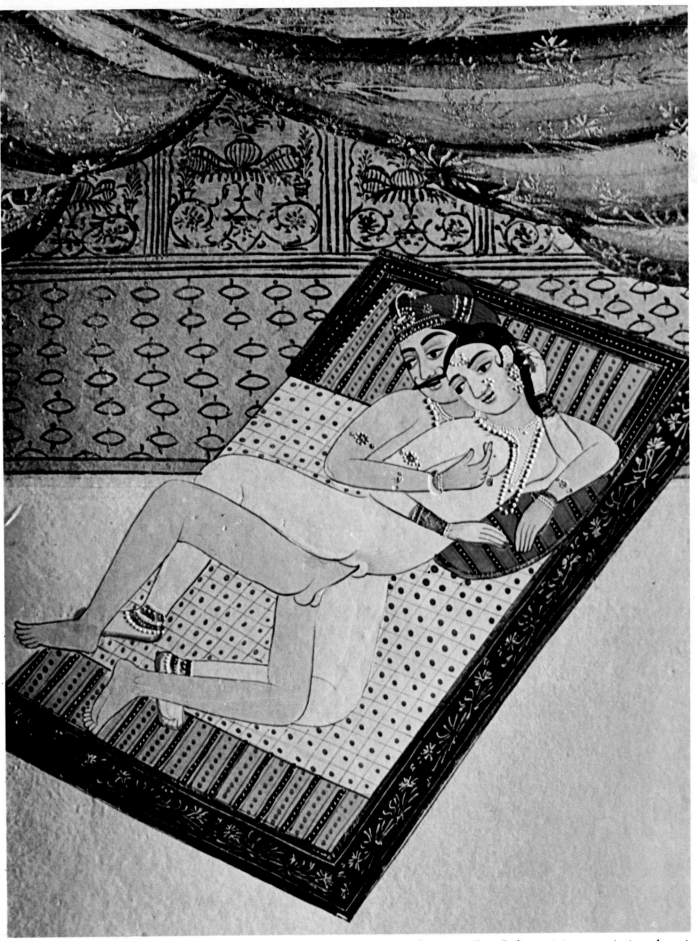

The 19th-century East Indian miniature painting above is part of a series made to illustrate a position in the famous love book of India, the KAMASUTRA. The artist is believed to have been a native of Jaipur. This school of painting began in the 18th century but extended to the 19th.

103

Well-dressed Persian lovers seem to be flying away on a magic carpet in this delicate pencil drawing. Tenderness is indicated by the left hand of the man on the woman's head and her right hand on his hip, but these seem to be the only evidences of love or passion that are portrayed in the picture.

In this extremely well-executed Persian painting the artist has intensified the feeling of movement in his swirling treatment of the man's shirt, the woman's pubic hair, and their headgear. The leaves on the tree add a touch of light delicacy and a feeling of impetuosity to this painting.

THE 20th CENTURY

The 20th century may easily become known as the century in which true sexual freedom came within the grasp of everyone. Not that everyone is willing to accept this freedom, but the philosophers, scientists, artists and writers have laid a solid foundation for a new view of human sexuality.

Each new generation, in coping with the frustrations inherent in survival, finds ways to make survival more viable, to make it a more enjoyable experience. Instinctive sexual reflexes of men and women supply important and basic gratification. But sexual satisfactions also come from learned responses. People add to the strictly physical act of sex through their visualization and fantasies of it, allowing sexual experiences without physical participation. This spirit of joy in the physical aspects of sex was never completely extinguished by the church or state. Yet it was not until the 20th century in Europe and in North America that freedom to see, as well as freedom to read and to think, became a human right.

It seems incredible that within 70 years so much cultural acceleration has separated sex from superstition, mythology and religion, and has placed sexual enjoyment at the top of the legitimately recognized pleasures available to everyone. The group of scientists and artists responsible for this reversal may seem to us to have been a permanent part of our culture. Yet it was only yesterday, in the present century, that the works of Krafft-Ebing, of Sigmund Freud, of Havelock Ellis made sex respectable. Other early explorers of the 20th century include the French writers Colette (Sidonie Gabrielle Colette), Théophile Gautier and Honoré de Balzac; James Joyce of Ireland and D. H. Lawrence of England; and such artists as Bonnard, Toulouse-Lautrec, Picasso, Duchamp and Miró.

Krafft-Ebing in Germany, the first great sexologist, spent his adult life researching and analyzing sexual aberrations. His pioneering laid open many of the dark mysteries of so-called aberrant sexual behavior. Sigmund Freud in Austria went many steps deeper into human sexuality. He advanced the theory that memories buried within the subconscious mind were often impossible to reach except through dreams and fantasies, that through analysis of such dreams, it was possible to understand and correct them. Thus aberrant behavior, once understood, could then be translated into normality. This, of course, was also the basis for the Surrealist movement in art. Havelock Ellis in England was a physician-psychologist. In his massive seven-volume *Studies of the Psychology of Sex*, he examined sex from both the scientific and the esthetic viewpoints. Borrowing from Freud, he moved into the subconscious mind by analyzing his own dreams.

It is doubtful that erotic paintings imported from Asia had any effect on early 20th-century erotic painting in Europe. Ideas regarding sexuality had long outstripped the stage of development at which China, Japan, India and Persia had become frozen. But as erotic art died in the Orient, it continued to expand endlessly in Europe, like the lingam, the phallus of the creator of the Hindu world. An interesting example of this Oriental-Occidental contrast concerns the nude figure. By the time the naked figure had become recognizably human in Europe, it was banned completely in Japan. As European artists began to show the under-the-surface sensuality and the reality of male and female bodies, the Orient completely rejected them. Throughout the entire 20th century, and even now, the nude figure cannot be shown in Japan either in paintings or in the flesh. At a recent Picasso exhibition in Tokyo, almost a

An early 20th-century orgy, "The Age of Gold," painted by André Masson. Masson insisted upon calling his early works automatic drawings, works that moved directly from his subconscious mind to brush and canvas. He did not believe in either editing nor stopping, once he began a painting.

third of the paintings were censored by the government because male or female genitalia were exposed. In Japan distributors of foreign magazines and even art books employ hundreds of workers to stamp ink blots over exposed penises or vaginas. Not a single pubic hair is allowed to be visible.

It took a long time for women to appear nude in the theaters of Europe. When one finally did, about 1910, she had been transformed from a living being to an inanimate piece of decoration. For naked men or women were allowed only to appear as living statues—sometimes as part of huge vases, often with flowers intertwined, and always standing in classic poses. Censors considered the bare breast and bare ass acceptable as long as they did not move.

The same brand of prudery still occurs in some of the mass media of the U.S. and Europe. There have been exhibitions of erotic art in many major capitals, but pictures from these exhibitions are frequently discarded entirely or cropped by the major newspapers and magazines, which are still careful not to offend the organized guardians of morality.

Yet one of the major victories over prudery in Europe and in the U.S. has been the elimination of precensorship. In the 17th, 18th and 19th centuries the works of a writer or an artist could be condemned before being published or exhibited. The work was not judged on its merits nor on its artistic or educational value. The government simply confiscated whatever erotic works could be found, and their creators were fined or jailed. Today our courts have decided that art is of value to society and that erotic art has a place in the total scheme of things. In the recent history of censorship, although courts sometimes rule against a work and suppress it, decisions have been overwhelmingly in favor of allowing adults to see and read what they wish. If Fanny Hill went to court today, she would most likely be considered an underprivileged girl with voyeuristic leanings and mild nymphomania. Casanova and Don Juan, rather than sexual criminals, would more likely be adjudged compulsive playboys. And both Leopold Sacher-Masoch and the Marquis de Sade would be advised to get psychiatric help.

The traditional guardians of morality, church and state, have been so beleaguered by the great artists and writers (and even the not so great) that censorship began to lose ground early in the 20th century, and even though a new conservatism attempts to impose restrictions on painting or writing from time to time, the masses of people have had a taste of sexual freedom, like it—and show no inclination toward giving it up.

In this sketch book of erotic painting the emphasis is not upon styles or schools of painting but on content. But there is no way to define the content of erotic art, any more than it is possible to define that of erotic writing or erotic architecture. There is only art. It is pleasurable, or stimulating or repellent. And each viewer must ultimately judge for himself whether the artist has successfully transferred an experience to him. It would be best if critics would get away from putting labels on paintings, for there is always a danger that from erotic art we could come to erotic outdoor art, erotic homosexual art, black erotic art, male erotic art and female erotic art. What we label erotic art is art that reflects human sexuality, art that involves the deepest passions of which humans are capable. And so far, erotic art seems to be the best name we have found for it.

In the first quarter of the 20th century a series of art disciplines developed that were to shake the very foundation of art, erotic and otherwise. The first of these was called Dada and it meant just what it sounds like: nonsense. The painters who came together to form this school were led by Marcel Duchamp, who not only electrified the art world with "Nude Descending a Staircase" but continued with such irrational and outrageous works as "The Passage from Virgin to Bride" and "Bride Stripped Bare by Her Bachelors." It was not easy to find the bride, the virgin or even the nude in these examples of Dadaism, yet they were vaguely erotic, for considerable direct sexual imagery and symbolism were involved in them. The nonsense aspect of this discipline had to do with the irrationality of living in a world involved with the first World War. The Dadaists said, in effect, that no art they could create

A deeply devout man who is best known for his stained-glass-window-like paintings of Christ, Georges Rouault departed from his usual somber style in painting this gay dancer. Although the lady wears stockings and blouse, the painting gives the impression that she is naked underneath her skirt.

could be as nonsensical or as radical as people killing one another in large numbers each day. The artists were working toward an intellectual explosion that would shock the public into consciousness of the irrational aspects of the world.

The Dadaist movement was short-lived. Surrealism picked up the pieces of Dadaism and reconstructed a new and stronger art discipline out of them. Like Sigmund Freud, whom they accepted as a confrere, the Surrealists set themselves to describe the aberrations and fantasies of mankind. Because such dreams were rooted in sexuality, most Surrealist painting had erotic aspects. Some painters such as André Masson and Dali used easily recognizable erotic symbols. Max Ernst and René Magritte were more subtle, yet erotic images are important in many of their works. Juan Gris, Marc Chagall, Paul Klee and Joan Miró used romantic symbols, yet eroticism dominates many of their canvases.

André Breton was the most articulate spokesman of Surrealism (the name coined by Guillaume Appolinaire). In the Surrealist manifesto published in 1924, Breton defined it:

SURREALISM. noun, masculine. Pure psychic automatism, by which one intends to express verbally, in writing or by any other method, the real functioning of the mind. Dictation by thought, in the absence of any control exercised by reason, and beyond any aesthetic or moral preoccupation.

With Surrealism as its father and the comic strip as its mother, Pop art was born in England in the late 1950s. It quickly spread to the U.S., and in these two countries it thrived. Like other art disciplines, much of Pop art had erotic aspects. Outstanding artists of the Pop school included Allen Jones, Richard Hamilton and Peter Blake in England; Larry Rivers, Tom Wesselmann and Andy Warhol in the U.S.; and Kurt Schwitters in Germany. But if these artists were pioneers of Pop art, their development did not stop there. They went on to outgrow the Pop movement.

The Pop school itself does not concern us, but the factors that joined together in creating it do—for advertising art, comic strips, folk art and fine art were all fused into this new movement. It became a fresh and imaginative aspect of art, which utilized contemporary images. But Pop art did more than infinitely multiply Coca-Cola bottles or give birth to Campbell soup cans. The best artists of this period saw the commercial exploitation of sexuality and created yet another way of viewing sexual behavior. Pop art offered more to erotic painting than this, however. It reflected the knowledgeability and uncomplicated acceptance of varying forms of sexual imagery, commercial as well as non-commercial. But, as in the case of the Romantic, Impressionist, Post-impressionist, and Surrealist movements, the school as such faded away and only the great painters that emerged from it remained on the scene.

Erotic art moved closer to reality, though keeping some commercial aspects of Pop art in a movement known as New Realism. The artists of this school projected themselves into a realm of absolute realism, with slices of contemporary life, including the erotic, scientifically viewed. The aim of this school was to achieve realism beyond that of the photograph. Its art reflects both the growth and decay of real objects. As the mobile society that it records has continued to move west, a high percentage of New Realism painting comes from the western region of the United States, where such artists as Duane Hanson, Mel Ramos, John de Andrea and Robert Bechtle live. But, although this movement seems new, it is certainly as old as Gustave Courbet, Balthus and the realistic Dutch masters of the 16th century.

Painters of the New Realism are by no means the first to look to photography as a realistic base for painting. But even this movement is beginning to give way to freer and less rigid visualizations of civilization. As society changes, art will continue to change with it—and to lead it in new directions. As the sexual and economic roles that men and women play continue to change, art will continue to reflect the changes. As alterations occur in the status of humans, the eye of the artist is ever on them. He will stay ahead of the viewer of his works, ever breaking new visual ground—ever explaining, entertaining and educating society's eye and helping to free it from inhibitions.

After experimenting with Cubism and early Surrealism, René Magritte went his own unique way as an artist. All of his works use recognizable objects that are juxtaposed in astonishing ways. In another version of this famous "portrait" called "Le Viol" or "The Rape," the mouth is lacking hair.

A scene in a Paris brothel that catered to unusual tastes shows a shy transvestite being exhibited by the madame to two clients. Like Lautrec, Jules Pascin (Julius Pincus) spent much time portraying habitués of MAISONS CLOSES, the brothels of France. His erotica often dealt with depravity.

With pixieish delight, Federico Castellon of Spain has conceived and drawn a most erotic quartet. In the sensual specifics he has included fellatio, sodomy and a heterosexual embrace. The gnome-like figures that appear in most of Castellon's erotic works add a decadent aura to these scenes.

An extraordinary draftsman with a distinctive style, the Italian artist Capuletti in this drawing emphasizes sex by directing the eye unerringly toward the genitalia. Although only a minor part of his output was specifically erotic, all of his paintings were influenced by his sensuous approach.

"The Guitar Lesson" is one of the few erotic oil paintings made by Balthus, who usually worked in pencil. In this shocking scene, Balthus has placed the hand of the teacher to direct the eye of the viewer to the young girl's vulva, and has led the eye to the teacher's breast with the pupil's left hand.

Sensual women are at the center of most of the compositions of painter Paul Delvaux. Although often painted in a classical style and in

eamlike setting, the women are always human. They give the impression of still life paintings that are waiting for the action to begin.

A recent Delvaux shows a distinct change in style. This lesbian motif, slightly reminiscent of "The Sleep" by Gustave Courbet, shows two activ

assionate women making love. The technique is freer, the women less classical than in the work on the preceding page, painted 20 years earlier.

Two drawings by André Masson reveal his extraordinary ability to use the so-called automatic technique. Like 15th-century Zen Buddhist drawings, these are made in pen and ink with an almost continuous line. In both cases the artist has fashioned spacious landscapes out of human sexuality.

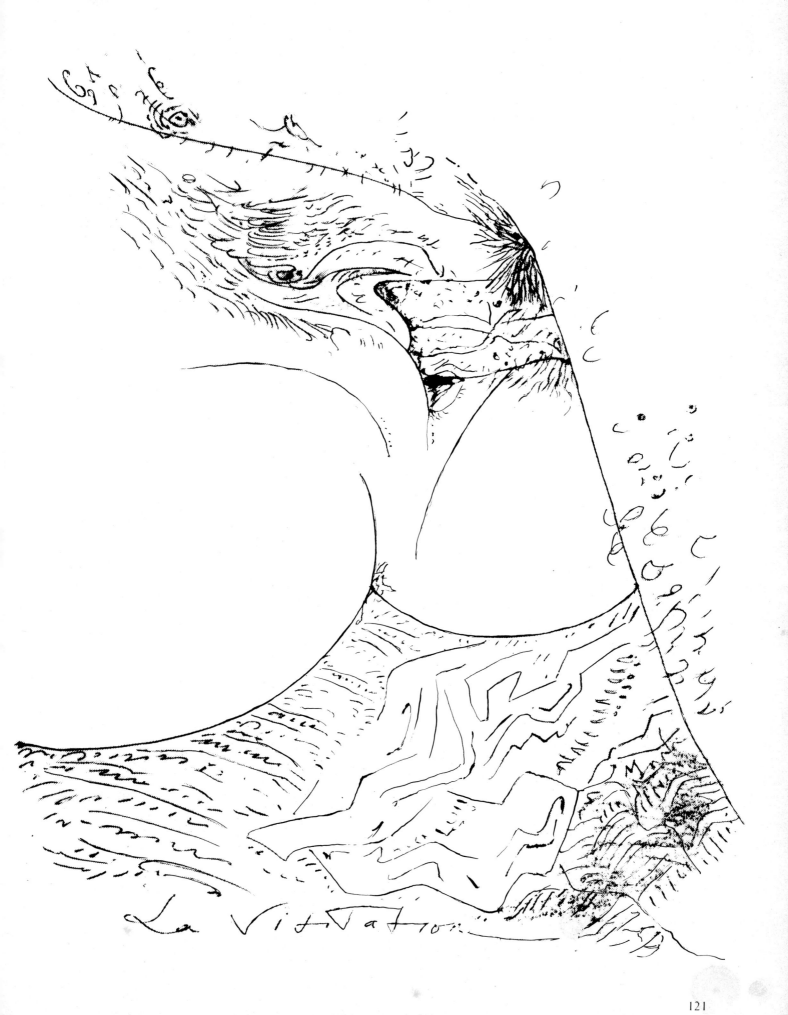

La Visitation

121

The ancient Greeks believed that eating the flower or fruit of the lotus plant brought forgetfulness and dreamy contentment. In this Pop art treatment, the French artist Gadal has created an erotic design out of the lotus leaf and the stamen, and has transformed a woman into the lotus blossom.

This late night fantasy painted by A. Reiss shows a surprise encounter with a cat woman as she is shedding her outer skin. Although the styles are entirely different, the theme is the same as that used in some early Japanese folk paintings, in which cats are shown transforming themselves into women.

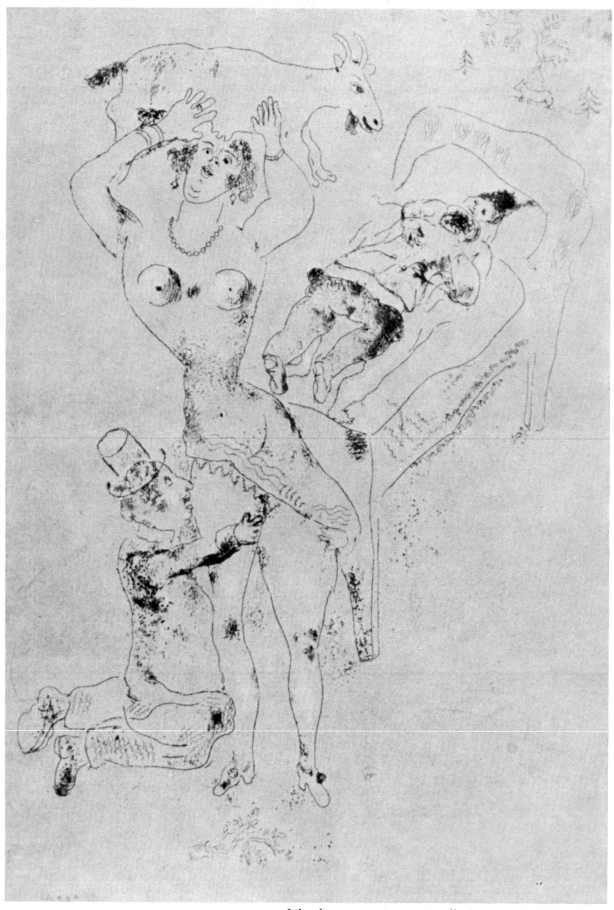

Like almost every internationally famous artist, Marc Chagall has painted some erotic pictures. This signed lithograph is typical of the dreamlike projections of his later paintings. It has much of the ritualistic, poetic and ethnic flavor that is characteristic of his better-known lithographs and paintings.

Mutual sexual satisfaction is the theme of this whimsical primitive painting by A. Fassianos. The participants are a well-dressed gangster and his nude girlfriend. The raw brilliance and extreme contrast of the colors used by the artist in this work make the figures glow as brightly as neon lights.

124

Two romantic, sexually symbolic images flank this classical nude painted by Michel Desimon. In the left foreground is a conch shell, long a symbol for the female vagina, and in the background is a labyrinth where paradise can only be reached after a long search through the maze—to its heart.

A modern Venus seems to be rising from the sand in this romantic fantasy by Bernard Louédin, the French painter of many erotic works. To enh

sensuousness of the scene, the featureless head is encased in a vulva-like shell, while two other shells symbolic of phalli appear in the foreground.

Representative of the modern
school of sentimental erotic
painting is this idyllic view of
sexual love, titled "The Burning Bush." Jean Paul Cleren has
effectively combined the outdoor feeling of leaves, bushes
and trees in the hair of both the
man and woman, and has
given both of them roots as well.

Among the most popular and distinctive painters of semi-clothed women is France's Roland Bourigeaud. His women look as though they are well-dressed even when they are partially nude. Bourigeaud seems to realize how important clothing is to women, and he successfully blends two themes.

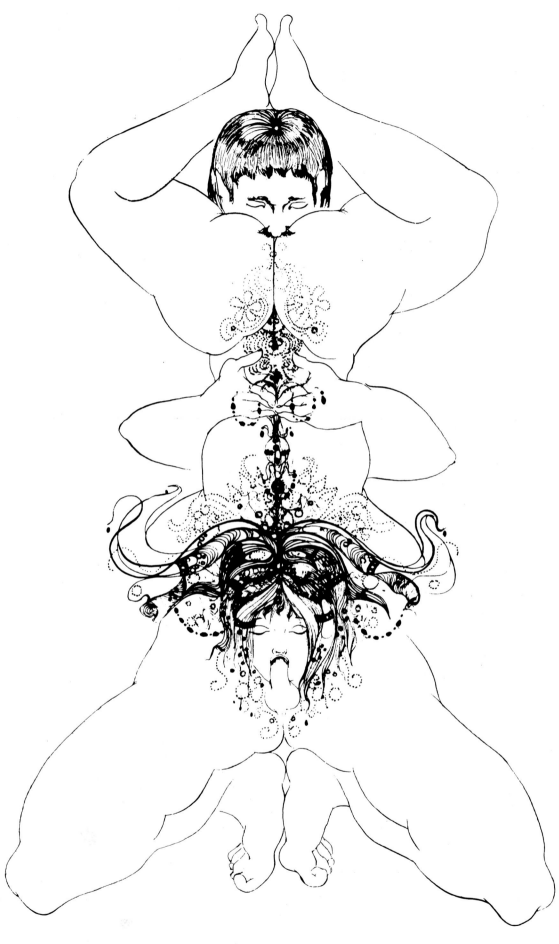

Above, the French painter Didier Moreau has created a decorative design utilizing the theme of SOIXANTE NEUF. At
right, the artist Moarch Eveno has encased the figure of a
nude woman within a fish. This painting, which is on wood,
is titled "Le Poisson de Profondeurs" ("The Fish of the Deep").

A favorite erotic theme from the 17th century onward has been the temptation of St. Anthony. This drawing by Stefan Zechowski is a rare 20th century interpretation. At right: the great surrealist master Salvador Dali's drawing of the female genitalia is a subtle masterpiece of eroticism.

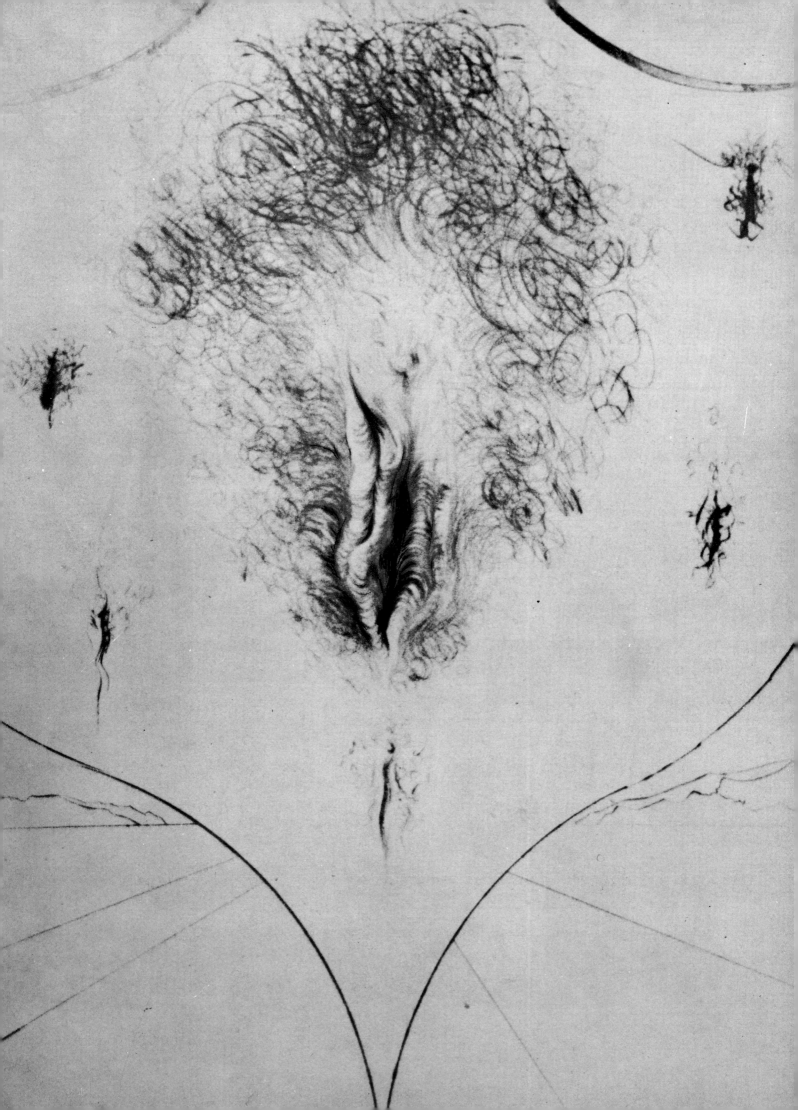

4.9.68.I

25.6.68.III

A master of the erotic theme, as he was of many themes and styles, Pablo Picasso did his most erotic series of drawings in 1968 at the age of 87. This period includes the finest of the master's erotic works, yet he exhibited another erotic series painted when he was 90. Artists seen with their models, bearded bull-like satyrs and women accompanied by sailors were favorite subjects to be interpreted in Picasso's free style.

12.5.68.
II

139

"St. George Fighting the Octopus" is one of Salvador Dali's recent erotic works. The octopus with its multiple penises seems to have ravished the maiden but St. George fights on, trying to reach the malignant eye of the monster. Dali has a long history of Surrealistic-erotic works. One of his best-known paintings, now in the Hugh Hefner collection, is the large canvas reproduced at the right, which is titled "Young Virgin Autosodomized by Her Own Chastity." Although Dali was not one of the pioneer Surrealists, from 1930 to the present he has been the dominant figure of the movement.

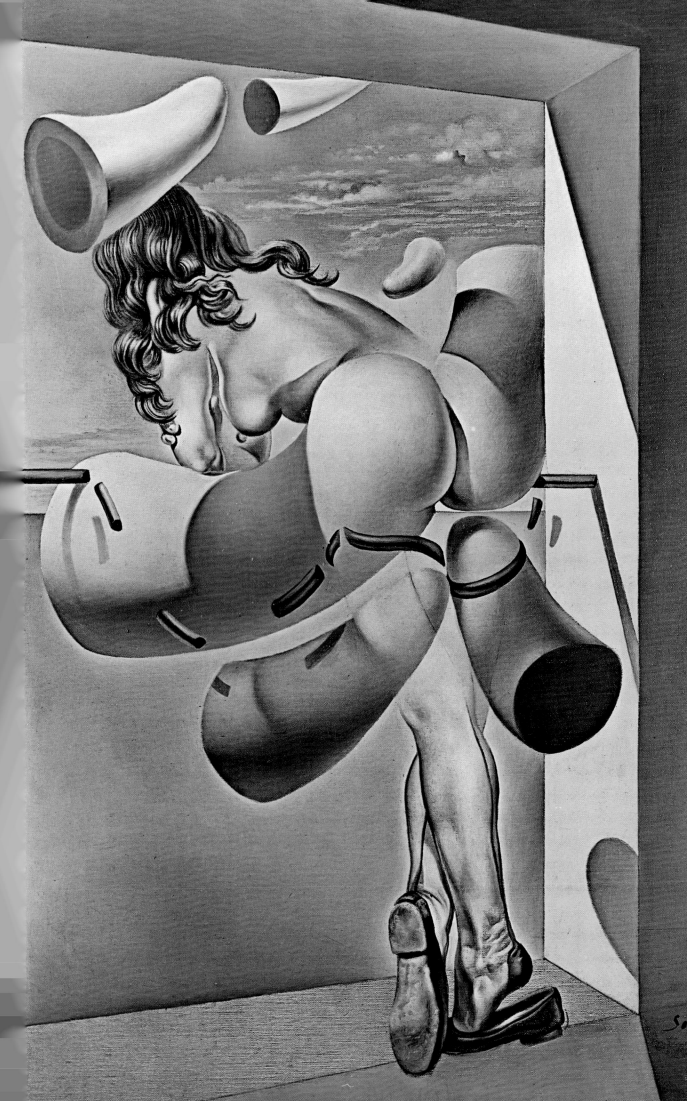

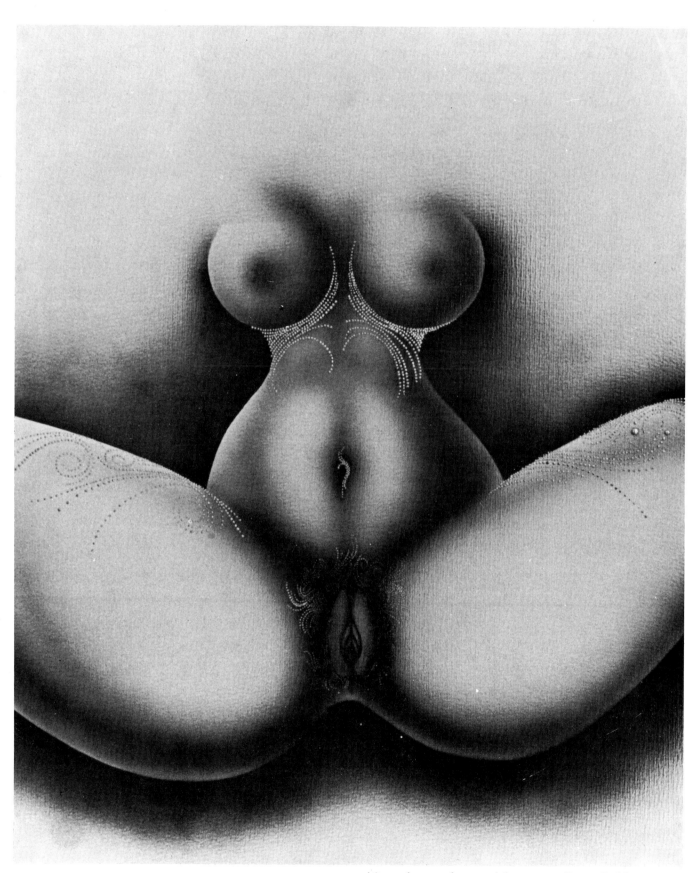

After a long and successful career in Paris, Roldàn, a specialist in erotic works, painted in Spain and has now moved on to Italy. His whirls and circles form designs that are based on female anatomy. Lace-like decoration, which contrasts with the geometrical precision, is typical of Roldàn.

144

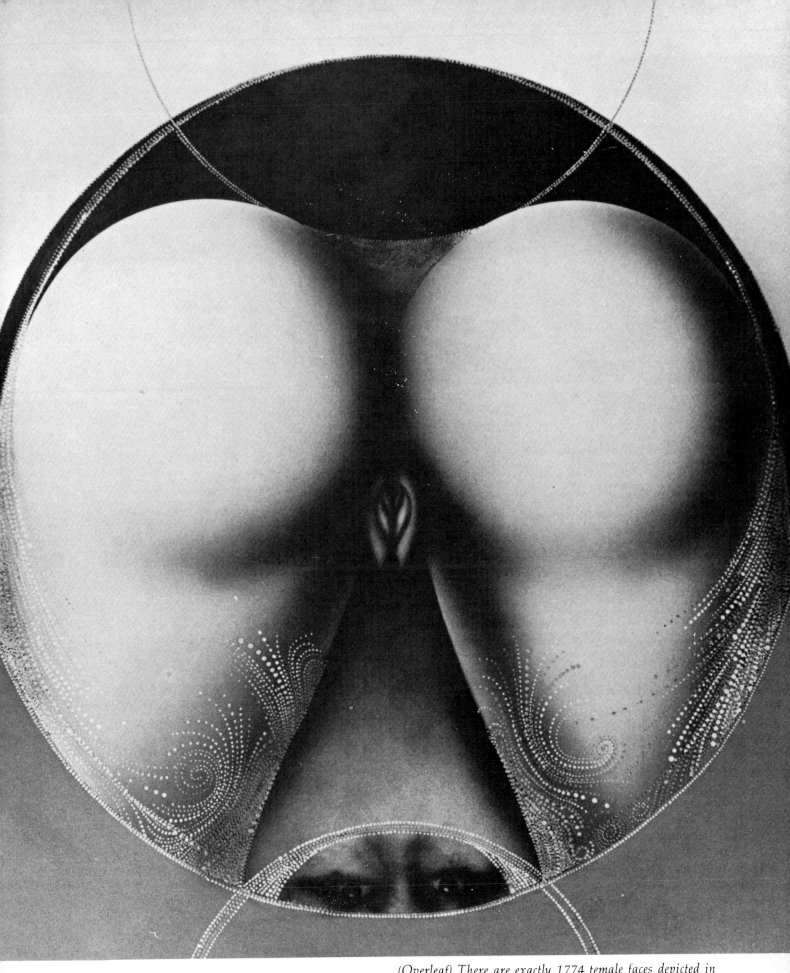

(Overleaf) There are exactly 1774 female faces depicted in ecstasy that make up this semi-abstract yet erotic design by the West German artist, Thomas Bayrle. It is one of a series of erotic pattern lithographs created by Bayrle in 1972.

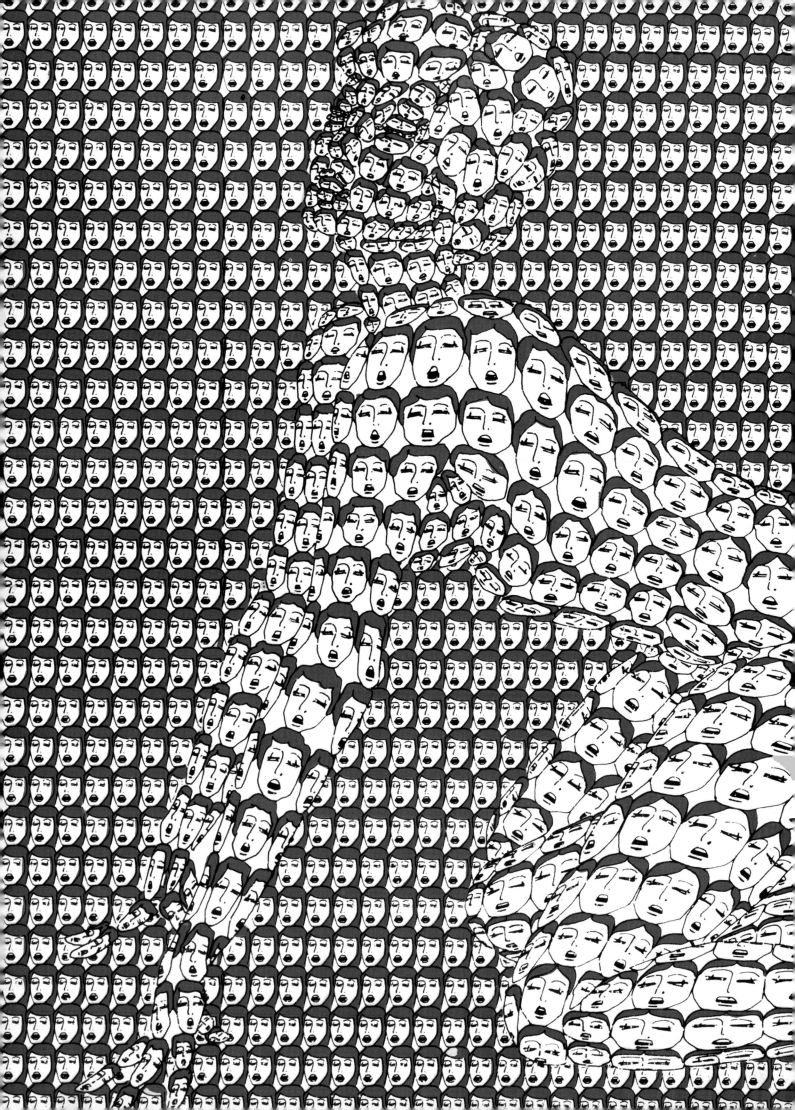

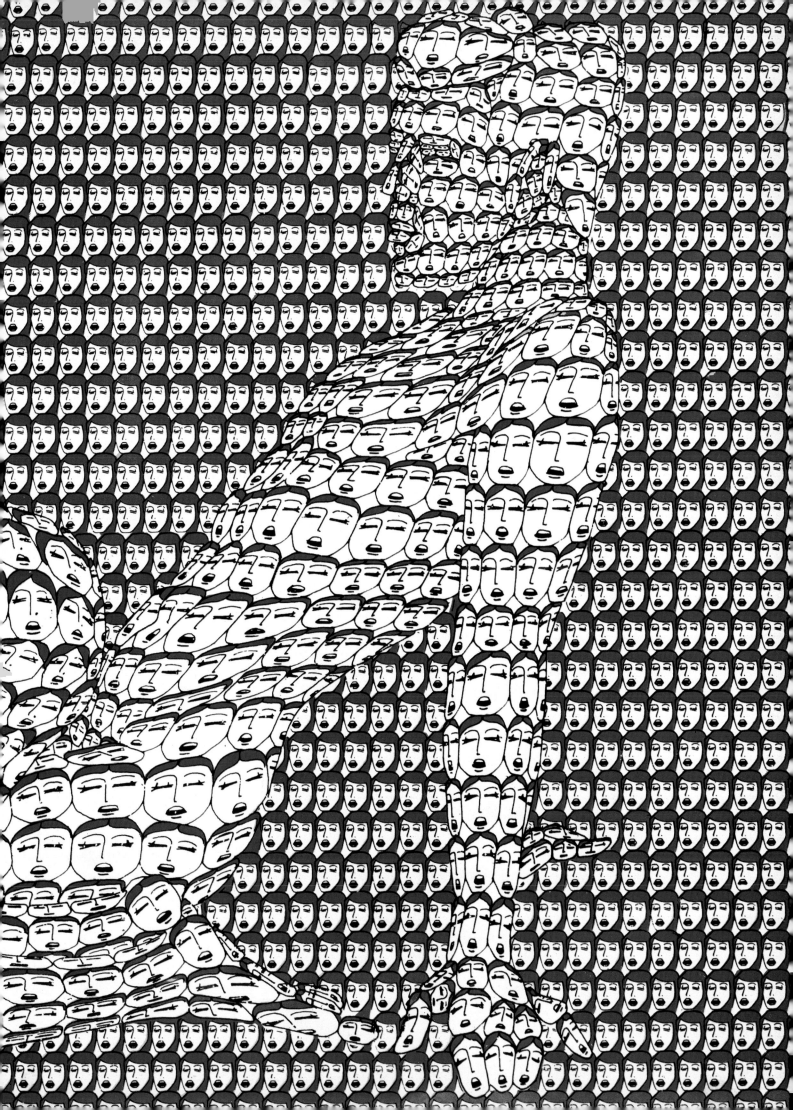

Born in Panama, Julio Zachrisson has since become one of Spain's best-known etchers. In the etching of the lesbians shown above, he has combined realism with compassion. At the right is an example of one of Zachrisson' more bizzare concepts, in which fantastic animals are seen as phallic symbols.

The most prolific of 20th-century erotic artists is Hans Bellmer of France. An early Surrealist, Bellmer has continued to
delve into the subconscious mind, creating sensual images
that are shocking and at times terrifying. Both male and female organs emerge, in the complex interaction of subjects.

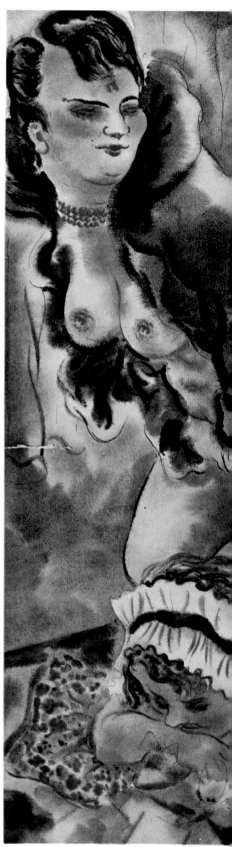

These caricatures satirizing the sexual appetite of humans
were painted in the 1920s by the German artist George
Grosz. Like Daumier, Grosz was a satirist, an artist, and a
critic as well. The figure at the right with the exaggerated
erection is Grosz's self-portrait of himself as a participant.

(Overleaf) One of Europe's great masters and leader of the
Fantastic-Romantic school is Dr. Ernst Fuchs of Vienna,
Austria. Fuchs has long been enchanted by visions of the
sphinx. Here he has painted her in a mysterious locale. With
one hand she holds her breast, with the other hand a phallus.

Controstworbation
par
la femme

GROZ

Drawn late in his life, this pen-and-ink sketch by Grosz shows more compassion than he usually displayed in his earlier works. A phallic candle lights the scene as a woman with gargantuan thighs, her dress pulled up above her waist, is masturbating a man whose fingers are rigid in ecstasy.

Refinement of technique and of sentiment is reflected in this erotic drawing by the Viennese artist Gustav Klimt. Klimt, who was at the height of his fame during the early years of the present century, skillfully used the clothing of his models to enhance the overall erotic effect, rarely revealing them nude.

157

This disturbing nude was painted by the Viennese artist Egon Schiele in 1917, a year before his death at the age of twenty-eight. Emotional stress, a component of all his paintings, is here visible in the nervous outline of the figure, the clenched fingers and the wrinkled sheet. Schiele's more decorative early paintings were influenced by Gustav Klimt, a leader in the Art Nouveau movement; but by the age of twenty, Schiele had embarked on his own very personal style.

The neurotic technique of Egon Schiele is evident in this drawing of two girls. Recognized by only a few avant-garde artists, Schiele led a lonely life and was once arrested for painting erotic pictures. He proudly admitted to being guilty as charged, and was sent to prison for nearly a month.

This tortured figure of a man with an erection is a self-portrait painted by Schiele near the end of his short life. After ten years of financially unrewarding effort, Schiele had an exhibition in 1918 that was a complete success. But the artist did not live to enjoy it. He and his wife died in that year.

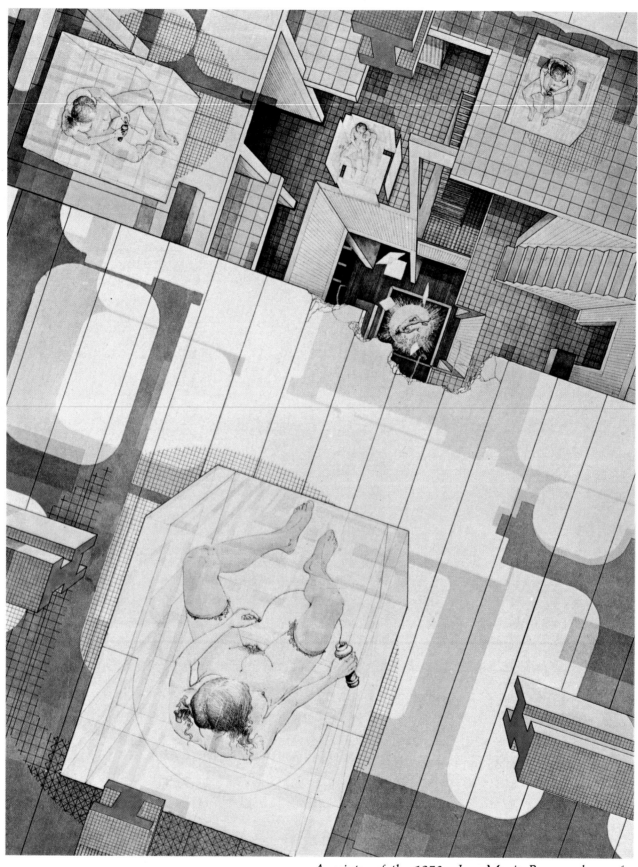

A painter of the 1970s, Jean-Marie Poumeyrol goes far beyond sex in its simple forms. In the painting above, the artist's X-ray vision penetrates an ultra-modern apartment building, revealing women in their bathrooms who are engaged in titillating themselves with a variety of vibrators.

The slow decay of an old schoolroom, the private "kept-after-school boredom," the carnal atmosphere created by two overripe young girls—all of these elements contribute to the erotic feeling that is expressed by Poumeyrol in the carefully composed and meticulously painted scene reproduced here.

162

Sexual symbolism is at the center of all of the works of Jean-Marie Poumeyrol. But in addition to symbols he uses satire and familiar objects to obtain his striking erotic effects. Both plumbing and voyeurism also play an important part in the highly detailed compositions of this important French artist.

The innocent appearance of the pubescent girls, and the contrast with the gigantic Dürer-like horse and its huge sexual organs, combine to shock the mind into remembrances of the sexual fantasies of childhood. The fearful but unidentifiable growths at the lower left of the picture add to the total impact.

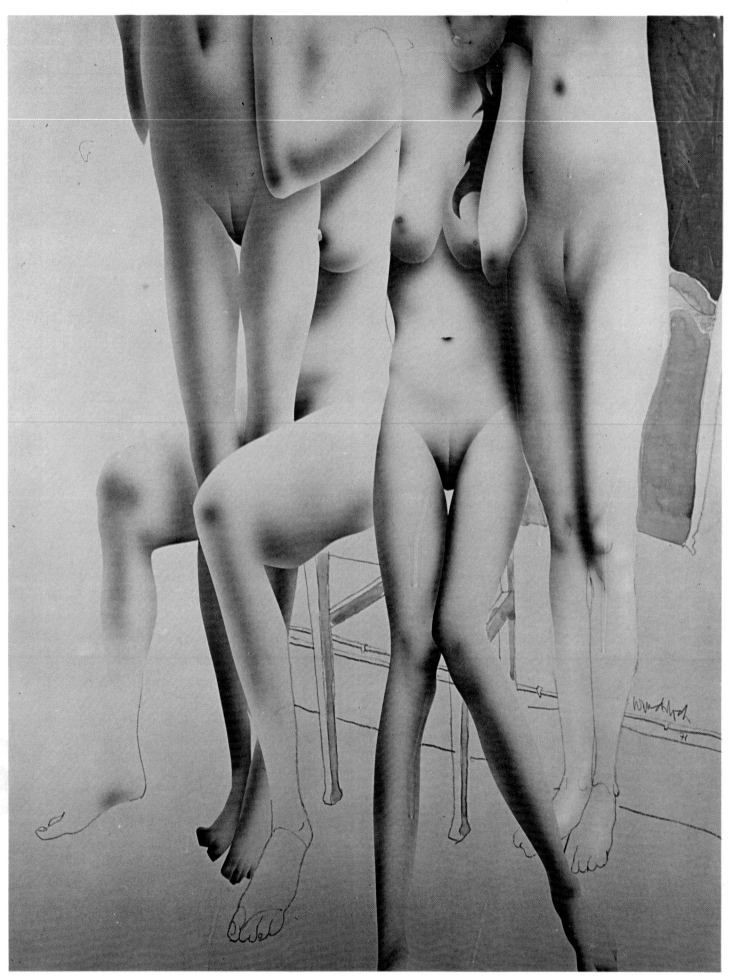

The women in Paul Wunderlich's erotic paintings belong to the 60s and 70s. They are slim and small-breasted, with carefully groomed hair and hands. Although sexually interesting, his nudes are usually painted without pubic hair, as above. This gives them a mannequin-like appearance.

Echoes of the Renaissance and the Baroque era are combined
with modern discipline in the individualistic erotic paintings
of Louis de Wet. Born in South Africa, this artist now paints
in London. The erotic effect in de Wet's painting emerges
from the strong contrast between ancient and modern forms.

Although de Wet works from live models, they are only a
framework from which his paintings unfold and develop. His
finished work uses symbols such as leaves and fronds rather
than realistic genitalia. In the picture shown on the right, the
split heart emphasizes the heart-shaped vulva of the girl.

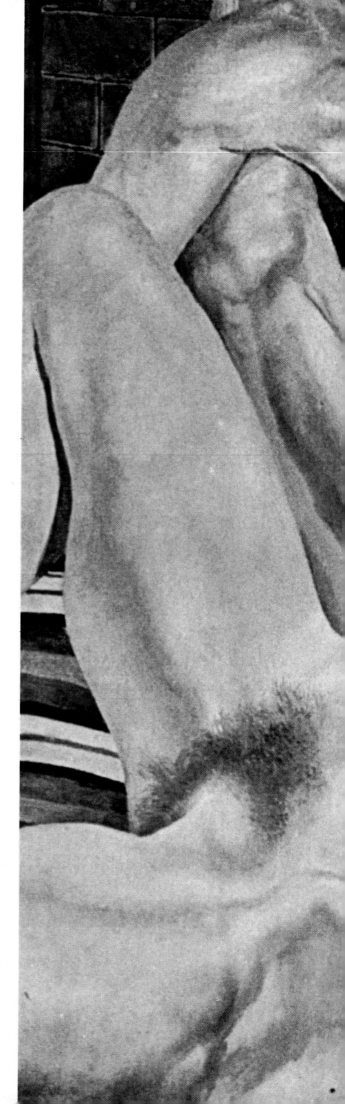

The erotic interest of the artist is combined with a realistic approach, creating a warm effect in this revealing self-portrait of the distinguished English artist Sir Stanley Spencer and his second wife. Adding to the "at home" atmosphere is the brightly glowing stove and the uncooked leg of mutton.

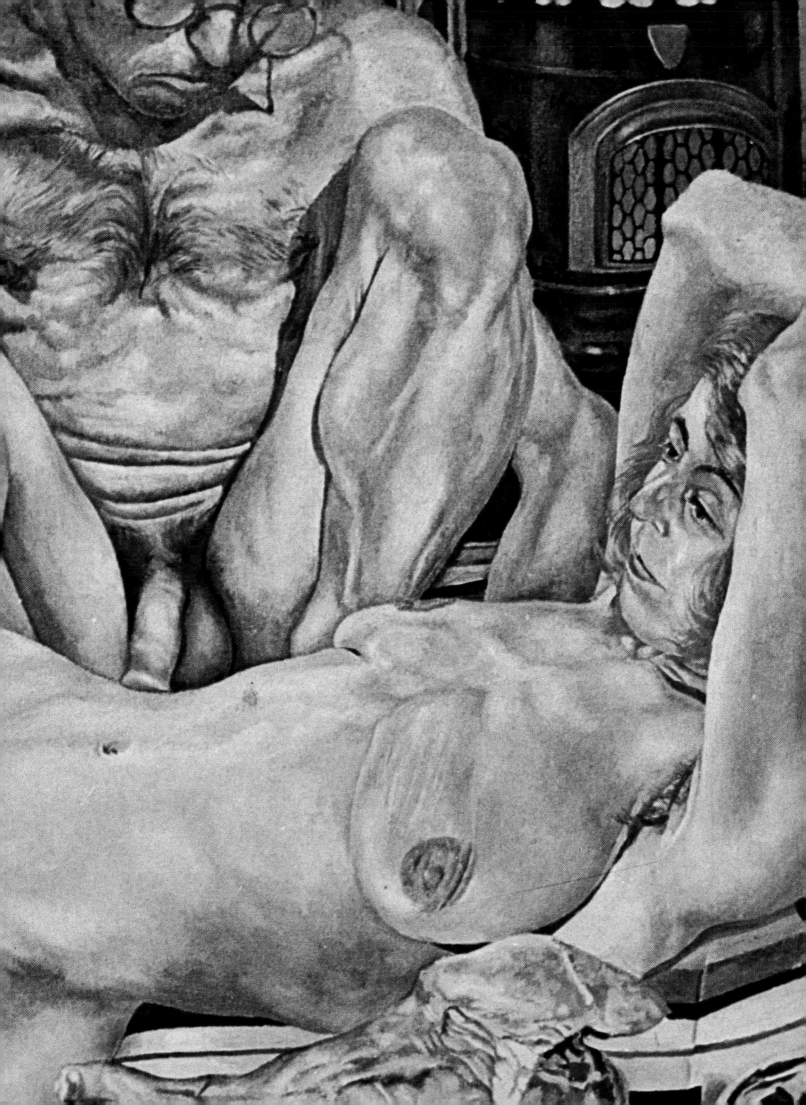

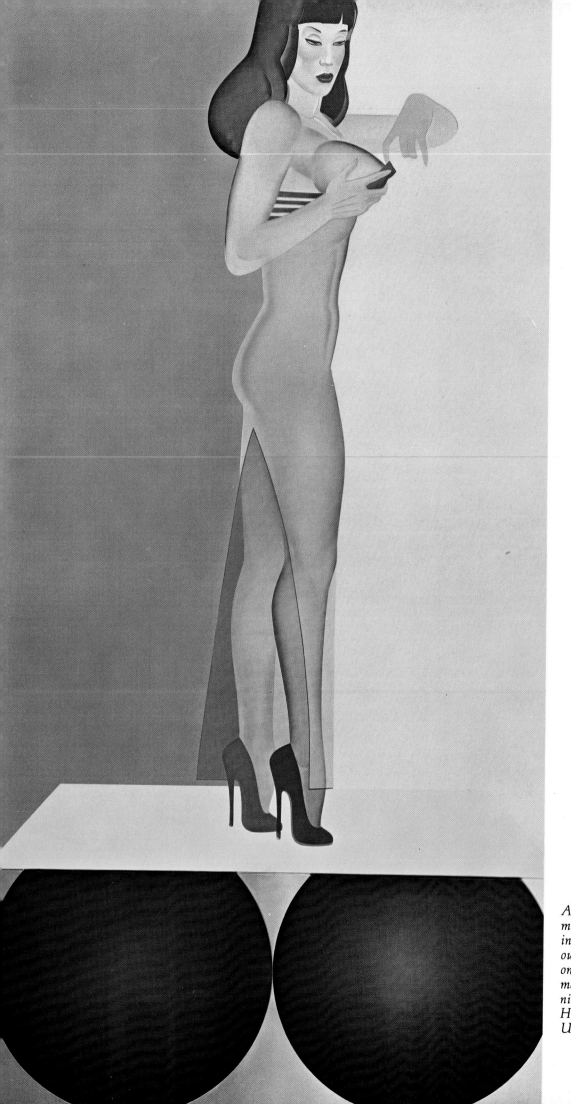

An effective joining of male and female sexual symbols is visualized in these paintings by Allen Jones, outstanding English artist. Jones, once identified with the Pop art movement, has created a special niche in the world of modern art. He is exhibited widely in the United States and also in England.

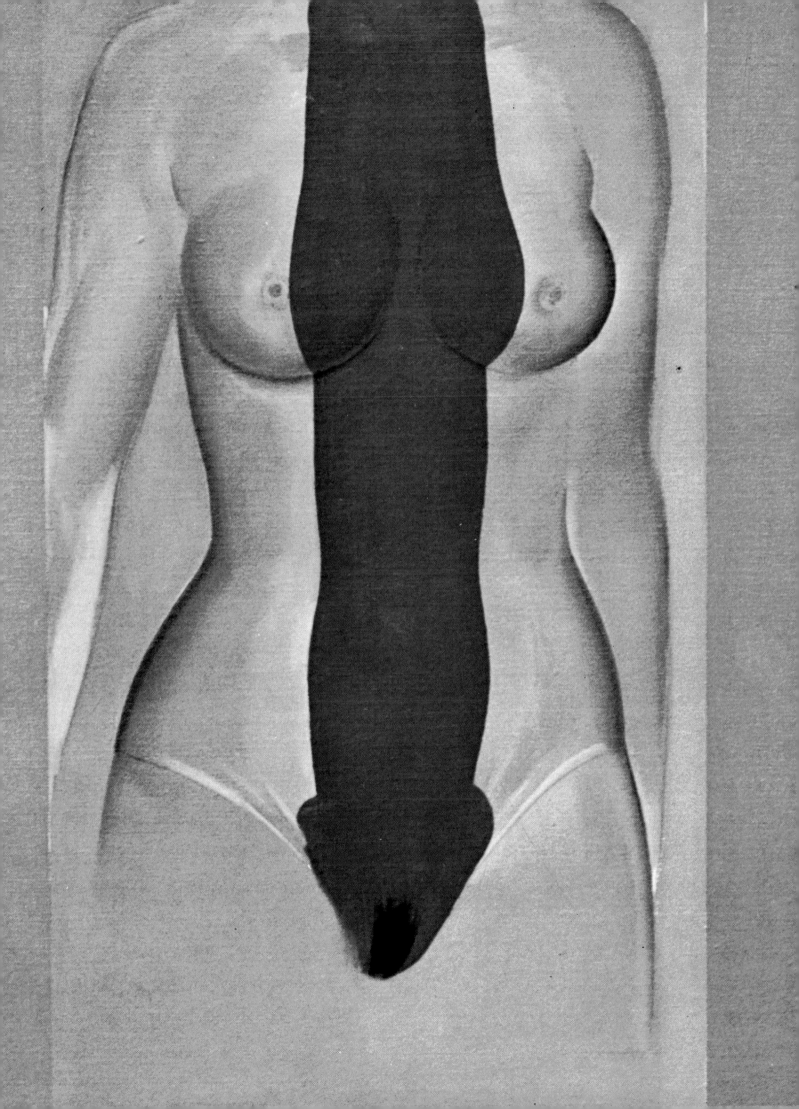

Considered the most erotic artist now painting by some critics, Graham Ovenden specializes in the Lolita image. Here he shows budding sensual

n two panels, leaving the third—the future—to the viewer's imagination. A meticulous artist, Ovenden is unable to meet the demand for his works.

In the 20th century women began to paint erotic subjects. The picture above, "Amerika: Love It or Leave It" by Harriette Frances, is a colored etching painted in 1971. Although Miss Frances' style is original, it shows the influence of the Pop Art movement and the early works of Tom Wesselmann.

Greatest of all the women erotic illustrator painters was Clara Tice, whose work appeared in many fine erotic editions during the second and third decades of this century. The illustration at right is a watercolor painted for a privately printed edition of MADEMOISELLE DE MAUPIN in 1927.

Tom Wesselmann, always interested in fine art, has recently moved toward fine erotic art. A new Wesselmann is an event in museum circles. "Bedroom Painting #20" is at top left; below, the original sketch for "Great American Nude #87," which made erotic art history. The pencil sketch was a gift to his close friend, the Chinese artist Walasse Ting.

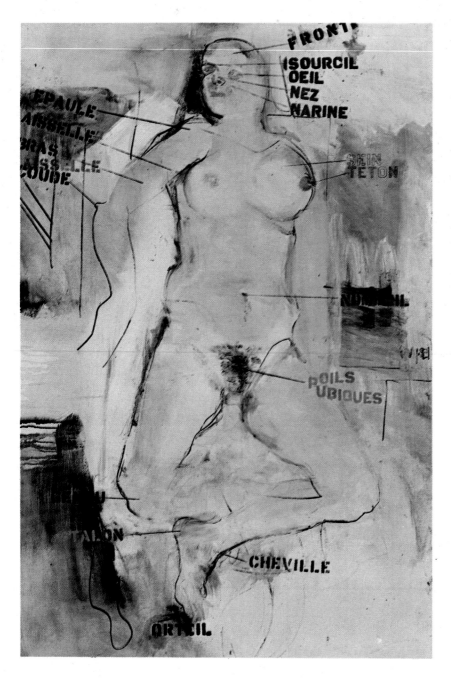

Another outstanding American artist who has a fine-art approach to eroticism is Larry Rivers, whose work has influenced the English Pop movement although he has never been part of it. Rivers' themes are usually American, but in the nude above various languages describe the girl's anatomy.

In a spoon-like back to front embrace, Morton Kaish has painted two lovers. The mixed media painting is called "Odalisques." Kaish has handled the design and color in such a way that the viewer must use his imagination to determine the sex of the person who is lying behind the woman.

The automobile takes on phallic significance in this sun-nude-mobile society painting by Dan Douke, southern California artist. The almost lifesize acrylic work is satirically titled AUSTIN HEALY SPRITE, ETC., the naked etc. dominates the painting. It is representative of the New Realism school.

This amusing contrast, with Bridget O'Murphy painted by François Boucher at the top and a beautiful woman who strikingly resembles actress Ursula Andress below, is called "Touché Boucher." Mel Ramos began painting characters from comic books but developed a distinctive art style.

184

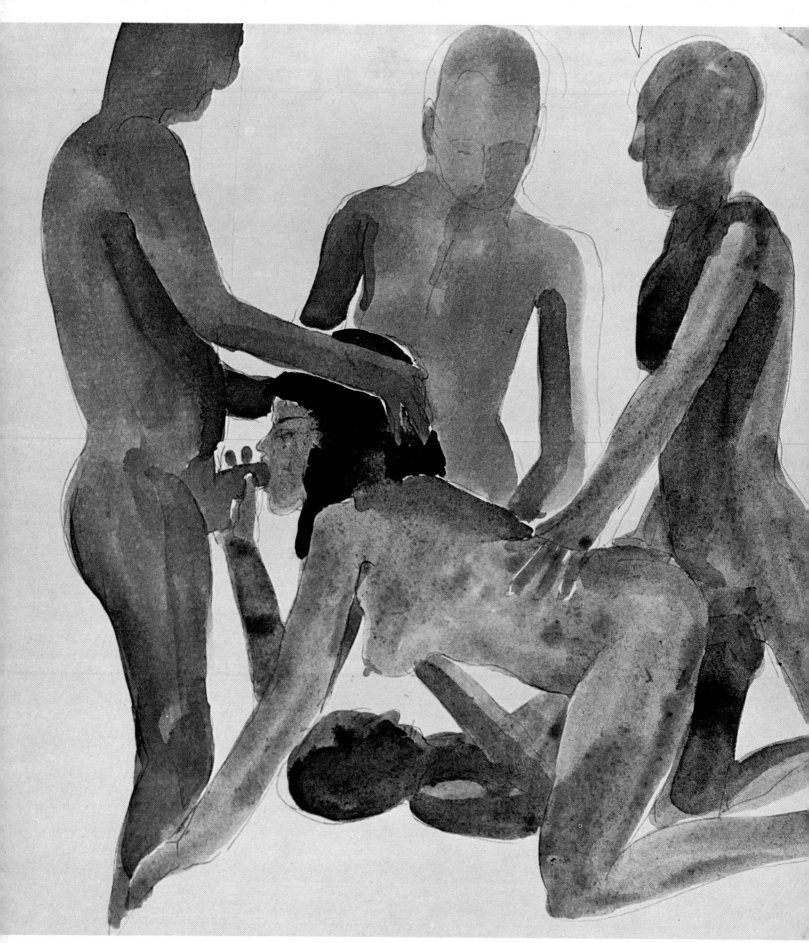

Using a free watercolor style slightly reminiscent of the sketches of Rodin, Robert Andrew Parker shows promise of becoming one of the great erotic artists of the 20th century. With a great economy of line and color, Parker nonetheless manages to make his subjects seem solid and recognizable.

(Overleaf) Almost breathing statuary is the work of John de Andrea, who works from photographs and live models, producing his sculpture to scale. His radical New Realism, part of the complexity of our ultra-realistic culture, has strong connections with such painters as Fuseli and Courbet.

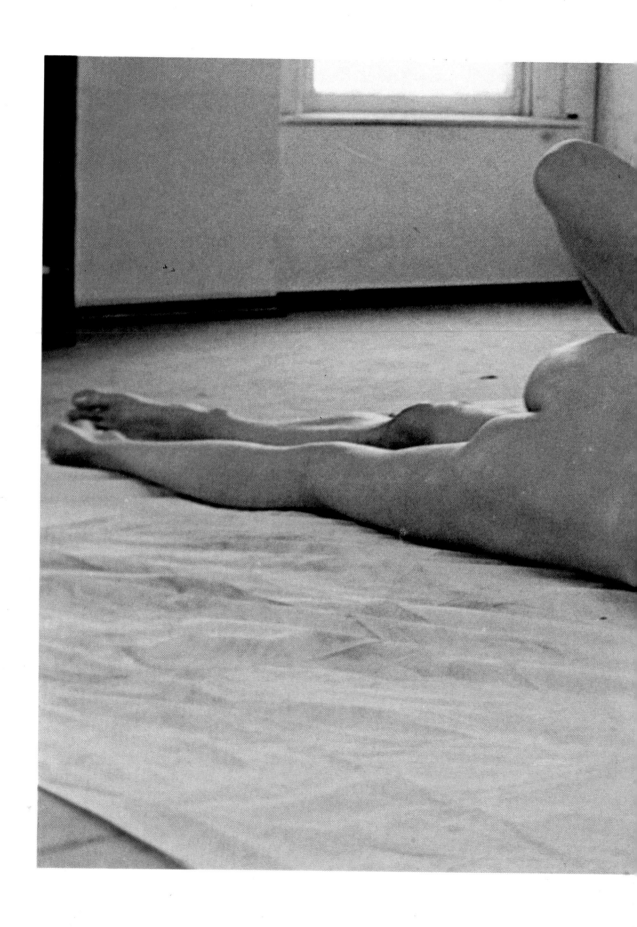

One of the great American artists of the 20th century, Willem de Kooning often uses sexual symbols in his paintings, and these devices have also appeared in the sculptures that he has recently exhibited. In the canvas shown here, form, color and exaggeration contribute to total erotic effect.

Simply and classically painted, this compassionate work by Robert Broderson is called "Embrace." It has the direct impact of some of the equally shocking "Horrors of War" etchings created by Goya. Yet the painting dramatically reveals to the viewer the universal human need for love and affection.

(Overleaf) Out of the comic book, extending beyond earlier conventional Pop art, Martha Edelheit, a young New York artist, has created a modern version of the painter David's "Rape of the Sabine Women." This watercolor is titled "The Albino Queen and Snowwhite Dream of Battle."

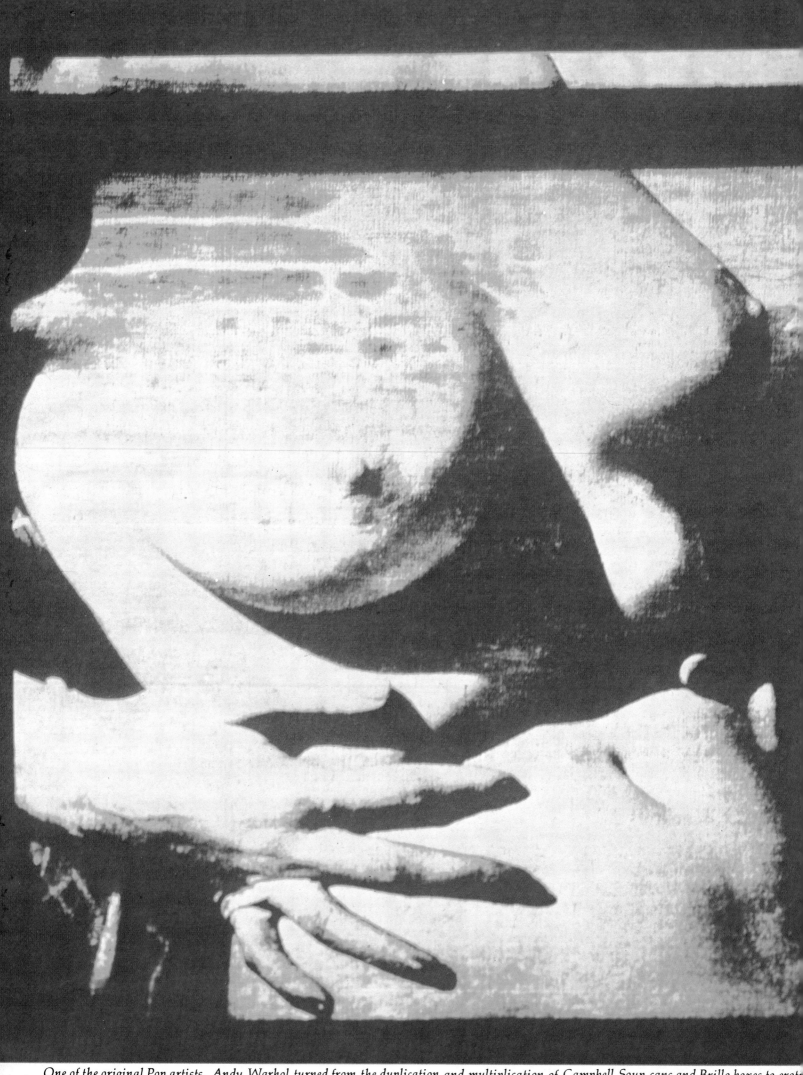

One of the original Pop artists, Andy Warhol turned from the duplication and multiplication of Campbell Soup cans and Brillo boxes to erot

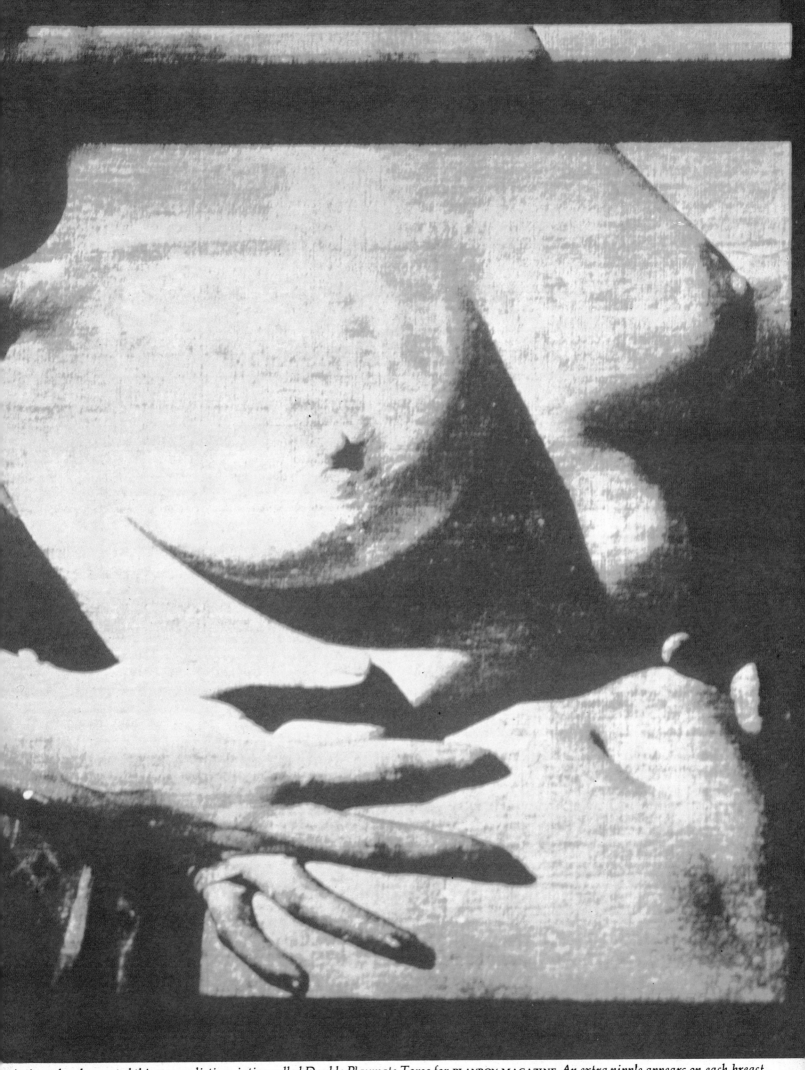

painting when he created this neo-realistic painting called Double Playmate Torso for PLAYBOY MAGAZINE. *An extra nipple appears on each breast.*

This intimate and affectionate bas relief was created by George Segal, who was associated with the Pop movement but moved to a modern romantic classical style. Once a student of abstract expressionist Hans Hoffman, Segal broke away because of interest in painted and sculptured figures.

Acknowledgments

A book is never created without the assistance of many people, and *EROTIC ART OF THE MASTERS: 18th, 19th and 20th Centuries* is no exception. I wish to gratefully acknowledge the cooperation of two friends without whose assistance and counsel this work would not have been possible—Dr. Lawrence Gichner of the Gichner Foundation for Cultural Studies in Washington, D.C., and Dr. J. M. Lo Duca, distinguished publisher and editor in Paris.

I am equally grateful to Dr. Paul Mocsanyi, Director of The New School Art Center in New York, Victor A. Lownes of London, and Linda Watkins and Paul Gebhard of the Institute for Sex Research Inc. at Indiana University.

My thanks to the following friends and colleagues around the world who have given encouragement, advice and assistance.

IN THE USA: Henry Miller, Sidney Janis, S. L. Bergen-ACA Galleries, Phillip Bruno-Staempfli Gallery, Alison Burnham-Marlborough-Gerson Gallery, Patterson Simms-O.K. Harris Gallery, Captain Peter Moore, Jonathan Smith, John Waggaman, Carlos and Tove Dalmau, and French Reproduction Rights of New York.

IN FRANCE: Eric Losfeld, Jean-Luc Carbuccia, Jacqueline Demornex, Arielle de Corail, Adeline Cacan of the Musée de Petit Palais, Claude Aubrey, Rosaline Bacau of the Cabinet des Dessins the Louvre, Pierre Barousse of the Musée Ingres, Mlle. Marandet of the Bibliothéque Municipale and Monsieur de Grivel of Ville de Besançon.

IN ENGLAND: Victor Lownes, George Melly, Mme. Georgette Magritte, and Derek Bayes.

IN GERMANY: Thomas Bayrle.

IN SWITZERLAND: Gérard Nordmann

IN SPAIN: Salvador Dali, José Hernandez and Sharon Smith Hernandez.

IN INDIA: Durgapratap Singh.

IN JAPAN: Raymond Bushnell.

I am equally grateful to all the artists, collectors, and museums that have kindly allowed me to reproduce their works. Their names, gallery and museum affiliations will be found listed under *Works of Art* beginning on page 218.

Bibliography

Anand, Râj Mulk. *Kama Kala*. Geneva: Nagel, 1963.

Arson, Emmanuelle, *Dessins Erotiques de Bertrand*, ed. Eric Losfeld. Paris: Le Terrain Vague, 1969.

Bainton, Roland H. *The Horizon History of Christianity*. New York: American Heritage, 1964.

Benayoun, Robert. *Érotique du Surrealisme*. Paris: Pauvert, 1965. Bernier, Georges and Rosamond Bernier (eds.). *The Selective Eye*. New York: Random House, 1955.

Beurdeley, Michel, et. al. *Chinese Erotic Art*. Translated by Diana Imber. Rutland, Vermont and Tokyo: Charles E. Tuttle, 1969.

Boeck, Wilhelm and Jaime Sabartés. *Picasso*. New York: Harry N. Abrams, n.d.

Borde, Raymond. *Dessins Érotiques de Jean-Marie Poumeyrol*, ed. Eric Losfeld. Paris: Le Terrain Vague, 1972.

Bouret, Jean. *The Life and Work of Toulouse-Lautrec*. Translated by Daphne Woodward. New York: Harry N. Abrams, n.d.

Bowra, C. M. *Classical Greece*. New York: Time, Inc., 1965.

Brusendorff, Ove. *Love's Picture Book: The History of Pleasure and Moral Indignation*. Vols. I, II, IV. New York: Lyle Stuart, 1969.

Burnham, Sophie. *The Art Crowd*. New York: David McKay, 1973.

Bushell, Raymond. *Collectors' Netsuke*. New York and Tokyo: Walker/Weatherhill, 1971.

Christie, Anthony. *Chinese Mythology*. Feltham, Middlesex, England: Hamlyn House, 1968.

Clark, Kenneth. *Looking at Pictures*. New York: Holt, Rinehart and Winston, 1960.

Compton, Michael. *Pop Art*. Feltham, Middlesex, England: Hamlyn House, 1970.

Daulte, François. *French Watercolors of the 19th Century*. Translated by Frances Bap and David Joyce. New York: Viking Press, 1969.

Fuchs, Eduard. *Die grossen Meister der Erotik*. Munich: Albert Langen, circa 1932-35.

Gerhard, Poul. *Pornography in Fine Art from Ancient Times up to the Present*. Los Angeles: Elysium, 1969.

Gichner, Lawrence E. *Erotic Aspects of Hindu Sculpture*. Washington: Lawrence E. Gichner, 1949.

Gimpel, René. *Diary of an Art Dealer*. Translated by John Rosenberg, New York: Farrar, Strauss and Giroux, 1966.

Goldwater, Robert. *Gauguin*. London: Thames and Hudson, 1928.

———. *Primitivism in Modern Art*. New York: Vintage Books, 1967.

Grosbois, Charles. *Shunga: Images of Spring*. Geneva: Nagel, 1965.

Guibbert, Jean Paul. *Leonor Fini Graphique*. Lausanne, Switzerland: La Guilde du Livre, 1971.

Hadas, Moses. *Imperial Rome*. New York: Time Inc., 1965.

Haftmann, Werner. *Painting in the Twentieth Century*. New York: Praeger, 1965.

Hearn, Lafcadio. *Japan: An Attempt at Interpretation*. New York: Grosset & Dunlap, 1904.

Hogarth. New York: Lear, 1947.

Huisman, P. and M. G. Dortu. *Lautrec by Lautrec*. New York: Viking Press, 1964.

Indian Miniatures: The Song Celestial or Bhagavad-Gitâ. Translated by E. Arnold. Paris: Éditions du Sud, 1968.

Janson, H. W. *History of Art*. Englewood Cliffs, New Jersey: Prentice Hall; New York: Harry N. Abrams, 1962.

Jelenski, Constantin. *Leonor Fini*. Lausanne, Switzerland: La Guilde du Livre, 1972.

Julien, Édouard. *Lautrec*. Translated by Helen C. Slonim, New York: Crown Publishers, n.d.

The Kama Sutra of Vatsyayana. Translated by The Hindoo Kama Shastra Society. Benares and New York: Society of the Friends of India, n.d.

Kronhausen, Phyllis and Eberhard Kronhausen. *Erotic Art*. 2 vols. New York: Grove Press, 1970.

Kultermann, Udo. *New Realism*. Greenwich, Conn.: New York Graphic Society, 1972.

Lal, Kanwar. *The Cult of Desire*. Delhi: Asia Press; Hyde Park, New York: University Books, 1966. (Text reprinted from original book by A. D. McDiarmid.)

Lane, Richard. *Masters of the Japanese Print*. Garden City, N.Y.: Doubleday, 1962.

Lewinsohn, Richard. *A History of Sexual Customs*. Translated by Alexander Mayce. New York: Harper & Row, 1971.

Lo Duca, J.-M. *Erotique de L'Art*. Paris: Le Jeune Parque, 1966.

———. *Histoire de L'Erotisme*. Paris: Le Jeune Parque, 1969.

Lucie-Smith, Edward. *Eroticism in Western Art*. London: Thames and Huson, 1972.

Marcadé, Jean. *Eros Kalos: Essay on Erotic Elements in Greek Art*. Geneva: Nagel, 1962.

———. *Roma Amor: Essay on Erotic Elements in Etruscan and Roman Art*. Geneva: Nagel, 1961.

Marks, Claude. *From the Sketchbooks of the Great Artists*. New York: Crowell, 1972.

Marti-Ibañez, Felix (ed.). *The Adventure of Art*. New York: Clarkson N. Potter, 1970.

Munsterberg, Hugo. *The Arts of Japan*. Rutland, Vermont: Charles E. Tuttle, 1957.

Nouveau Dictionnaire de Sexologie. Directed by J.-M. Lo Duca. Paris: Encyclopédie Françoise de Poche, 1972.

Penrose, Roland. *Picasso: His Life and Work*. New York: Schocken Books, 1962.

Plumb, J. H. *The Renaissance*. New York: American Heritage, 1961.

Rawson, Philip. *Erotic Art of the East*. New York: Prometheus Press, 1968.

Relouge, I. E. (ed.). *Masterpieces of Figure Painting*. New York: Bonanza Books, 1959.

Renoir, Jean. *Renoir, My Father*. Translated by Randolph and Dorothy Weaver. Boston: Little, Brown, 1962.

Richardson, E. P. *A Short History of Painting in America*. New York: Crowell, 1963.

Rubin, William S. *Dada, Surrealism, and Their Heritage*. New York: Museum of Modern Art, n.d.

———. *Miro in the Collection of The Museum of Modern Art*. New York: The Museum of Modern Art, 1973.

———. *Picasso in the Collection of The Museum of Modern Art*. New York: The Museum of Modern Art, 1972.

Schmidt, J. E. *Cyclopedic Lexicon of Sex*. New York: Brussel & Brussel, 1967.

Stern, Harold P. *Master Prints of Japan*. Ukiyo-e Hanga. New York: Harry N. Abrams, n.d.

Waldberg, Patrick. *Eros in la Belle Epoque*. Translated by Helen R. Lane. New York: Grove Press, 1969.

———. *Eros Modern Style*. Paris: Pauvert, 1964.

Zimmer, Heinrich. *The Art of Indian Asia*. 2 vols., ed. Joseph Campbell. New York: Pantheon Books, 1955.

Zwang, Gerard. *Le Sexe de la Femme*. Paris: La Jeune Paris, 1967.

Index

The Works of Art

The 18th Century

Europe

14 Anonymous West Indian folk artist (Guadeloupe), (c. 18th century), tinted lithograph. Collection of Gérard Nordmann, Geneva.

15 Anonymous French folk artist, (c. 18th century), tinted lithographs, (top) *An Italian Artist's Studio*. Collection of Gérard Nordmann, Geneva.

17-19 Thomas Rowlandson (1756-1827), untitled watercolors. Collection of Victor A. Lownes, London.

20-21 Anonymous English folk artist, (c. 18th century), hand colored engravings. Gichner Foundation for Cultural Studies, Washington, D.C.

China

23-25 Anonymous Chinese artists, (c. 18th century), painted on silk. Gichner Foundation for Cultural Studies, Washington, D.C.

26 Anonymous Chinese artist, (c. 18th century), carved bas-relief panel, ivory and sandstone. Private Collection.

27 Anonymous Chinese artist, Ching Dynasty, (c. 18th century), watercolor. Gichner Foundation for Cultural Studies, Washington, D.C.

29-31 Anonymous Mongolian artist, (c. 18th century), scroll. Gichner Foundation for Cultural Studies, Washington, D.C.

Japan

33 (above) Isoda Koryusai (active 1760-1790), *Nun with Lover*, colored woodblock print. Private Collection.

(below, left) Anonymous Japanese carver, (c. 18th century), netsuke; mother-of-pearl egg, which opens to reveal a Geisha in ivory and a Blackamoor in ebony. Collection of Cornelius Roosevelt, Washington, D.C.

(below center and right) Anonymous Japanese carver, (c. 18th century), netsuke; lacquer and ivory box and cover innocent on outside but not when opened. Collection of Raymond Bushnell, Tokyo.

34-35 Suzuki Harunobu (about 1725-1770), Shunga (woodblock print). Gichner Foundation for Cultural Studies, Washington, D.C.

36-37 Kitagawa Utamaro (1735-1806), Shunga (woodblock print). Gichner Foundation for Cultural Studies, Washington D.C.

India

39 Anonymous artist, Rājasthān India, (c. 18th century), gouache. Courtesy of Doris Weiner Gallery, New York.

40 Anonymous Indian artist, (c. 18th century), watercolor; picture-puzzle design of horse. Collection of Durgapratap Singh, Maharashtra, India.

41 Anonymous Indian artist, (c. 18th century), watercolor; picture-puzzle design of elephant. Gichner Foundation for Cultural Studies, Washington, D.C.

43 Anonymous artist, (c. 18th century), folk painting, Rājasthān, India. Collection of Durgapratap Singh, Maharashtra, India.

The 19th Century

Europe

45 Édouard Manet (1832-1888), *Le Dejeuner sur l'Herbe (Lunch on the Grass)*, oil. The Louvre, Paris.

47 Théodore Chassériau (1799-1856), *Apollon et Daphne (Apollo and Daphne)*, oil. The Louvre, Paris.

49 Jean Auguste Dominique Ingres (1780-1867), *Le Bain Turc (The Turkish Bath)*, oil. The Louvre, Paris.

50 Ingres, untitled sketch from personal sketchbook. Musée Ingres, Montauban, France. Photograph by Albert Ferlin.

51 Ingres, *Leda and the Swan*, from personal sketchbook. Musée Ingres, Montauban, France. Photograph by Albert Ferlin.

52 Ingres, *Cupid and Psyche*, pen and ink, from personal sketchbook. Musée Ingres, Montauban, France.

53 Honoré Daumier (1808-1879), untitled watercolors. Signed HD. Gichner Center for Cultural Studies, Washington, D.C.

54 Daumier, untitled watercolor, signed HD, à Louise. Gichner Center for Cultural Studies, Washington, D.C.

55 Daumier, untitled watercolor. Gichner Center for Cultural Studies.

56 Gustave Courbet (1819-1877). *L'Origine du Monde (Woman's Torso)*, oil. Prof. Hatvany, Musée de Beaux Arts, Budapest. Courtesy of J.-M. Lo Duca, Paris.

57 Courbet, *Le Sommeil (The Sleep)*, oil. Musée du Petit Palais, Paris.

58 Charles Édouard de Beaumont (1821-1888), untitled, oil. Collection of Victor A. Lownes, London.

59 De Beaumont, untitled, pencil and watercolor. Collection of Victor A. Lownes, London.

60-61 Hilaire Germain Edgar Degas (1834-1917), *La Fête de la Patronne (The Madame's Party)*, aquatint. Institute for Sex Research, Indiana University, Bloomington, Indiana.

62 (left, above) Degas, *On Attend les Clients (Waiting for Clients)*, monotype. Institute for Sex

Research, Indiana University, Bloomington, Indiana.

(left below) Degas, *Admiration*, monotype. Ducet Library, Paris.

62-63 Degas, untitled monotype zincograph. Bibliothèque National, Paris.

64 (above) Henri de Toulouse Lautrec (1864-1901), *Phallische Phantasie (Phallic Phantasy)*, pen and ink sketch. Private collection.

(below) Lautrec, pen and ink sketch. Courtesy of Lucien Goldschmidt, Inc., New York.

65 Lautrec, *Femme de Maison (Woman of the House)* or *Femme Tirant son Bas (Woman Drawing on Her Stocking)*, oil. The Louvre, Paris.

66 Paul Gauguin (1848-1903), *Culte Maori*, aquarelle. Cabinet des Dessins, The Louvre, Paris.

67 Franz Xaver Winterhalter (1806-1873), *Der Verräterische Wasserspiegel (The Treacherous Water Reflection)*, oil. Private collection.

68-71 Eugéne Le Poitevin (1806-1870), original lithographs from *Les Diableries Erotiques (The Erotic Devils)*. Collection of Gérard Nordmann, Geneva.

72 Jean François Millet (1814-1874), *Pair of Lovers*, black and white pencil drawing. Prof. Hatvany Musée de Beaux Arts, Budapest.

73 Millet, *Nymph and Satyr*, black and white pencil drawing, signed JFM. Private collection.

74 Achille Deveria (1805-1857), tinted lithographs for original edition of *Don Juan*. Collection of Gérard Nordmann, Geneva.

75 Attributed to Deveria, *The Harem*, tinted lithograph. Gichner Foundation for Cultural Studies, Washington, D.C.

76-77 Deveria, tinted lithographs for privately printed editions of *Gamiani* by Alfred de Musset. Collection of Gérard Nordmann, Geneva.

78 Constantin Guys (1802-1892), *Trio*, drawing. Courtesy of J.-M. Lo Duca, Paris.

79 Aubrey Vincent Beardsley (1872-1898), pen and ink illustration for *Lysistrata*. Private collection.

80 Michael von Zichy (1827-1885), black and white sketches. Gichner Foundation for Cultural Studies, Washington, D. C.

81 Von Zichy, *Etudes des Mains (Studies of hands)*, black and white sketch. Gichner Foundation for Cultural Studies, Washington, D.C.

82 Pierre Auguste Renoir (1841-1919), *Les Baigneuses (The Bathers)*, oil. The Louvre, Paris.

83 Pablo Ruiz Picasso (1881-1973), *L'Entreinte (The Embrace)*, oil, signed: A mon cher ami Guillaume Apollinaire-Picasso. Galerie Louise Leiris, Paris.

China

85 Anonymous Chinese artist, (c. 19th century) *The Philosopher*, watercolor. Gichner Foundation for Cultural Studies, Washington, D. C.

86 Anonymous Chinese artist, (c. 19th century), watercolor. Gichner Foundation for Cultural Studies, Washington, D. C.

87-89 Anonymous Chinese artist, Ching Loong Dynasty, from *Book of Spring Paintings*. Private collection.

90-91 Anonymous Chinese artist, (c. 19th century), watercolor. Gichner Foundation for Cultural Studies, Washington, D. C.

92-93 Anonymous Chinese artist, (c. 19th century), two scenes from Ming Dynasty novel *Chin P'ing Mei (The Golden Lotus)*, popular in 18th century, watercolor. Collection of Victor A. Lownes, London.

Japan

94 Kitagawa Utamaro (1753-1806), *Man and Woman*, Shunga (woodblock print). Private collection.

95 Anonymous Japanese artist, (c. 19th century), scroll of precoital, coital and postcoital positions. Institute of Sex Research, Indiana University, Bloomington, Indiana.

96-97 Utamaro, *Two Lesbians*, Shunga (woodblock print). Gichner Foundation for Cultural Studies, Washington, D. C.

98-99 Anonymous Japanese artist, (c. 19th century) Shunga (woodblock print). Gichner Foundation for Cultural Studies, Washington, D. C.

100 Katsushika Hokusai (1760-1849), *Lovers*, Shunga (color woodblock print). Lent anonymously.

India and Persia

101 Anonymous Indian artist, (c. early 19th century) Jaipur school of miniature painting, illustration from *Kama Sutra*. Gichner Foundation for Cultural Studies, Washington, D.C.

102 Anonymous Persian artist, (c. early 19th century) erotic miniature. Collection of Durgapratap Singh, Maharashtra, India.

103 Anonymous Indian artist, (c. early 19th century), Jaipur school of miniature painting, illustration from *Kama Sutra*. Collection of Shriman Rao Saheb Naharsinghji, Deograb, Rājasthān, India.

104 Anonymous Persian artist, (c. 19th century), untitled, pencil on paper. Institute for Sex Research, Indiana University, Bloomington, Indiana.

105 Anonymous Persian artist, (c.19th century), miniature

painting. Institute for Sex Research, Indiana University, Bloomington, Indiana.

The 20th Century

Europe

107 André Masson (1896-), *L'Age d'Or (The Age of Gold)*, watercolor. Courtesy of J.-M. Lo Duca, Paris.

109 Georges Rouault (1871-1958), *Tabarin*, oil. Musée d'Art Municipal Moderne, Paris.

111 René Magritte (1898-1967), *Le Viol (The Rape)*, oil. Collection of George Melly, London. Reproduced with permission of Mme. Georgette Magritte.

112 Jules Pascin [Julius Pincus] (1885-1930), *Brothel, with Transvestite*, etching. Private collection. Photographed by John Waggaman.

113 Federico Castellon (1914-1971), untitled color lithograph. Collection of Mrs. Hilda Castellon, New York.

114 Jose Manuel Capuletti (1925-), *Contemplation*, pen and pencil drawing. Courtesy of J.-M. Lo Duca, Paris.

115 Balthus [Klossowski de Rola] (1908-), *La Lecon de Guitare (The Guitar Lesson)*, oil. Courtesy of Lo Duca's *Les Larmes d'Eros* by Georges Bataille, published by Jean-Jacques Pauvert, Paris, 1961.

116-117 Paul Delvaux (1897-), *Le Train de Nuit (Night Train)*, oil. Collection of Victor A. Lownes, London.

118-119 Delvaux, *Two Women*, mixed media. Collection of Victor A. Lownes, London.

120 Andre Masson (1896-), *Terre Erotique (Erotic Land)*, India ink. Galerie Louise Leiris, Paris.

121 Masson, *La Visitation (The Visit)*, ink and colored pencil. Galerie Louise Leiris, Paris.

122 Moarch Eveno (1934-), *La Flamme (The Flame)*, oil. Courtesy of J.-M. Lo Duca, Paris.

123 Albert Reiss (1909-), *Rencontre, la Nuit (Encounter at Night)*, oil. Courtesy of J.-M. Lo Duca, Paris.

124 Marc Chagall (1887-), untitled etching. Private collection.

125 Alexandre Fassianos (1935-), *Erotiko*, watercolor on cardboard. Galerie 3 + 2, Paris.

126-127 Michel Desimon (1927-) *Les Labyrinthes* or *Les Biens de la Terre (Blessings of the Earth)*, oil. Courtesy of J.-M. Lo Duca, Paris.

128-129 Bernard Louedin (1938-), *Naissance de Venus (Birth of Venus)*, oil. Courtesy of J.-M. Lo Duca, Paris.

130-131 Jean-Paul Cleren (1940-), *Buisson Ardent, Pyracanthe (Burning Bush, Pyracantha)*, oil. Galerie Lambert Monet, Geneva.

132 Roland Bourigeaud (1920-), *Albane*, oil. Courtesy of J.-M. Lo Duca, Paris.

133 Bourigeaud, *Belle des Rocheuses (Women of the Rocks)*, oil. Galerie 3 + 2, Paris.

134 Didier Moreau (c. 1934-), *Haute Symétrie (High Symmetry)*, India ink. Courtesy of J.-M. Lo Duca, Paris.

135 Eveno, *Le Poisson des Profondeurs (Fish of the Depths)*, oil on wood. Courtesy of J.-M. Lo Duca, Paris.

136 Stefan Zechowski, *Saint Anthony*, charcoal drawing. Collection of J.-M. Lo Duca.

137 Salvador Dali (1904-), pencil and charcoal drawing. Private Collection, Paris.

138 Pablo Ruiz Picasso (1881-1973), lithographs. Galerie Louise Leiris, Paris.

139 Picasso, *Dancing Nymph and Satyr*, lithograph. Galerie Louise Leiris, Paris.

140-141 Picasso, *Man with Flute*, oil. Musée du Petit Palais, Geneva.

142 Salvador Dali (1904-), *St. George Fighting the Octopus*, oil. Collection of Carlos B. Alemany, New York.

143 Dali, *Young Virgin Autosodomized by Her Own Chastity*, oil. From the Playboy Enterprises Collection.

144-145 Modesto Roldan (1919-), untitled anatomy, gouache with airbrush and pen. Courtesy of the artist, Madrid.

146-147 Thomas Bayrle (1944-), colored lithographs. Private collection.

148 Julio Agosto Zachrisson (1920-), untitled engraving. Courtesy of the artist, Madrid.

149 Zachrisson, untitled engraving. Courtesy of the artist, Madrid.

150-151 Hans Bellmer (1902-), untitled etching. Collection of Mr. Daniel Tereshko, Pennsylvania. French Reproduction Rights, New York.

151 Bellmer, untitled colored lithograph. Collection of Victor A. Lownes, London. French Reproduction Rights, New York.

152 (left, above) George Grosz (1893-1959), untitled watercolor. Courtesy of ACA Galleries, New York.

152-153 Grosz, self-portrait, watercolor. Collection of Victor A. Lownes, London.

154-155 Ernst Fuchs (1930-), *Sphinx*, oil. Courtesy of the artist.

156 Grosz, *Masturbation par la Femme (Woman Masturbating)*, pen and ink drawing. Collection of Victor A. Lownes, London.

157 Gustav Klimt (1862-1918), *Embracing Couple*, pen and ink drawing. Courtesy of Galerie St. Etienne, New York.

158-159 Egon Schiele (1890-1918), *Reclining Woman*, oil. Marlborough Gallery of Fine Art, London.

160 Schiele, *Two Nudes*, pencil drawing. Marlborough Gallery of Fine Art, London.

161 Schiele, said to be self-portrait, oil. Collection of Victor A. Lownes, London.

162 Jean-Marie Poumeyrol (1946-), *La Maison de Verre (The Glass House)*, scratchboard with ink and gouache. Courtesy of J.-M. Lo Duca, Paris.

163 Poumeyrol, *Les Petites Filles Modèles (The Nice Little Girls)*, scratchboard with ink and gouache. Courtesy of J.-M. Lo Duca, Paris.

164 Poumeyrol, *L'Ours en Peluche (Cotton Bear)*, scratchboard with ink and gouache. Courtesy of J.-M. Lo Duca, Paris.

165 Poumeyrol, *La Causette (Small Talk)*, scratchboard with ink and gouache. Courtesy of J.-M. Lo Duca, Paris.

166-167 Paul Wunderlich (1927-), untitled, acrylic. George Staempfli Gallery, New York.

168 Louis de Wet (1930-), *Landscape with the Church of Saint-Michel in Dijon, Burgundy, a Ford GT, and an Isotta Fraschini Tipo 8*, oil and egg emulsion. Courtesy of the artist.

169 De Wet, *I've lost something, I don't know quite what; but I think you may have it, signed, a girl, IV*, oil. Courtesy of the artist.

170-171 Sir Stanley Spencer (1891-1959), *The Leg of Mutton Nude*, oil. Collection of Peyton Skipwith, London.

172 Allen B. Jones (1937-), untitled, oil. Courtesy of the artist.

173 Jones, sketch for unfinished drawing, oil. Courtesy of the artist.

174-175 Graham Ovenden (1943-), *The Swallows First Morning*, oil. Collection of Victor A. Lownes, London.

United States

176 Harriette Frances, *Amerika: Love It or Leave It*, 1971. Colored etching. Achenbach Foundation for Graphic Arts, San Francisco.

177 Clara Tice (dates unknown), watercolor illustration for privately printed edition of *Mademoiselle de Maupin*, by Theophile Gautier. Collection of Bradley Smith.

178 (above) Tom Wesselmann (1931-), *Bedroom Painting No. 20*, oil. Sydney Janis Gallery, New York.

(below) Wesselmann, *Study for Great American Nude No. 87*, acrylic. Collection of Victor A. Lownes, London

179 Wesselmann, *Nude Masturbation Drawing*, pencil drawing. Walasse Ting Gallery, New York.

180 Larry Rivers (1928-), *Parts of the Body—French Vocabulary*, oil. Marlborough-Gerson Gallery, Inc., New York.

180-181 Rivers, *Movie House*, mixed media. Marlborough-Gerson Gallery, Inc., New York.

182 Morton Kaish (1927-), *Odalisques*, mixed media. Photograph courtesy of George Staempfli Gallery, New York.

183 Dan Douke (1943-), *Austin Healy Sprite, Etc.*, acrylic. Jack Glenn Gallery, Corona del Mar, California.

184 Francois Boucher (1703-1770), *L'Odalisque*, oil. The Louvre, Paris.

184-185 Mel Ramos (1935-), *Touche Boucher*, oil. Galerie Bruno Bischofberger, Zurich.

186-187 Robert Andrew Parker (1927-), untitled watercolors. Courtesy of the artist.

188-189 John de Andrea (1941-), untitled, polyester and fiberglass. Courtesy Galerie de Gestlo, Hamburg.

190 Willem de Kooning (1904-), *Woman*, oil. Collection of Victor A. Lownes, London.

191 Robert Broderson (1920-), *Embrace*, oil. Terry Dintenfass, Inc., New York.

192-193 Martha Edelheit (1931-), *The Albino Queen and Snow White Dream of Battle*, watercolor and ink on rice paper. Courtesy of the artist.

194-195 Andy Warhol (1931-), *Double Playmate Torso*, acrylic and silk screen on canvas. Originally appeared in Playboy Magazine; copyright © 1967 by Playboy. Courtesy of Playboy Magazine.

196 George Segal (1924-), *The Embrace*, plaster bas relief. Collection of Carlos and Tove Dalmau, New York.